INTERNATIONAL GOURMET

ITALIAN COOKING
TUSCAN

Elizabeth Cornish

WARD LOCK

First published in paperback in Great Britain in 1990 by
Ward Lock Limited, Villiers House, 41/47 Strand,
London WC1N 5JE, a Cassell Company.

This edition published in 1993

Designed by Melissa Orrom.
Text filmset in Garamond Original by
M & R Computerised Typesetting Ltd.,
Grimsby.

Printed and bounded in Hong Kong by Colorcraft Ltd

ISBN 1 85079 198 8

CONTENTS

Acknowledgements

Inside photographs by David Burch

Home Economists – Lorna Rhodes
and Linda Fraser

Line drawings by Lorraine Harrison

The publisher would like to thank the
following for kindly loaning equipment for
photography:

Reject China Shop
Bella Figura
J. K. Hill
The Bramley Hedge Shop

Notes

It is important to follow **either** the metric
or the imperial measures when using the
recipes in this book. Do not use a
combination of measures.

All recipes serve four people, unless
otherwise specified.

INTRODUCTION

The region of Tuscany, dominated by the majestic town of Florence, is the heartland of Italy, and its cooking reflects Italy's best home cooking – simple and robust yet classic. Here the excellence of the ingredients is paramount, and, as in the rest of Italy, the cook knows that what is local is best.

This is partly due to historical factors, stretching back to 1861 when Italy was still a divided nation with each region a separate and fiercely patriotic state. The mountainous countryside presented a further barrier to unification, with the result that each region developed its own characteristic customs, including culinary ones.

Even today the preference for fresh local ingredients – a cabbage from the garden, a leg of pork from a trusted butcher – means that despite improvements in transport and communication, it would be unthinkable to eat a pizza outside Naples or an *ossobuco* outside Milan – unless, of course, you wanted to put up with second best. The tourist in Italy can be sadly disappointed if he insists on eating his favourite 'Italian food' without knowing exactly where it comes from. There is no such thing as 'Italian food', any more than there is 'European food'.

On a geographical level, a look at the Tuscan landscape gives further clues to eating habits. The field of a small Tuscan farmer will have rows of vines with corn growing in between them, and interspersed with the grey-green of an olive tree. Sometimes a pig, a cow and a handful of chickens will feed among the crops. Though there are increasingly fewer small farms of this character, the staples remain the same: bread from the corn, olive oil to flavour it and wine to drink.

In the kitchen garden grow artichokes and asparagus, spinach – which has come to be particularly associated with Florence; fennel, pumpkin, beans of all kinds, especially broad beans and the small white cannellini beans known locally as *toscanelli;* a warm southern array of courgettes, aubergines, peppers and garlic, a profusion of tomatoes and, perhaps most important of all, carrots, onions, celery and parsley. These last four, known as *odori,* are used together constantly, softened in olive oil, to provide a basis rich in flavour for many of the recipes of the region.

Beyond the kitchen garden and the cultivated farmland, the Tuscan hills provide their own nourishment in the form of game of all kinds. Partridge, pheasant, guinea-fowl, rabbit and hare and the occasional wild boar all find their way to the cooking pot. On his way back from the hills the hunter will pick a few sprigs of wild rosemary or other herbs to flavour his supper.

Other birds too are eaten in Tuscany – small hedgerow dwellers and songbirds that would never be found on British or American tables but which are as natural to the Tuscan diet as the larger wild creatures.

In the early autumn the hunter's zeal becomes almost fanatical with the onset of the mushroom season. Over a hundred varieties of edible mushroom can be gathered, including the exquisitely flavoured *porcini* (ceps). Laws limit the number of mushrooms that may be bagged on a given foray into the woods, and chemists provide an identification service should an unknown and potentially poisonous species be encountered.

Freshwater fish from hill streams are another delicacy, but seafish, as in the rest of Italy, are never found far from the coast, where they are eaten on the day of the catch. Inland fish eaters have to be content with *baccalà*, dried salt cod, or *stoccafisso*, wind-dried cod. The name 'stoccafisso' is Scandinavian, and refers to the sticks around which the fish is wound to dry.

On the coast, Livorno, or Leghorn, is famous for *Cacciucco*, a thick fish soup whose ingredients vary according to the day's catch. This is eaten with a little olive oil dribbled over and a quantity of coarse white Italian bread.

Bread is, in fact, eaten with everything in Tuscany – a small hunk is torn off and used as an edible piece of cutlery, with a fork or spoon in the other hand. Tuscan bread is made without salt. This is because unsalted bread keeps better – salt draws moisture, and bread a few days old begins to lose its freshness. This is, however, put to good use by the thrifty Tuscans who use such bread in a variety of delicious dishes, such as *Panzanella*, the soaked bread salad, and *Pappa col Pomodoro*, a bread and tomato soup. Additionally, a slice of dry bread can be rubbed with garlic, before being toasted and laid in the bottom of a soup bowl before the hot soup is poured on. Another favourite recipe is *Crostini.* These are squares of bread fried in oil or butter or baked with cheese, and used to garnish all manner of dishes.

When the bread is fresh, however, the best way of eating it is with a dribble of golden green olive oil (the best is said to come from Lucca) and a sprinkling of coarse sea salt. With a dish of young raw broad beans, some slices of peppery salami and a wedge of *pecorino* – the golden, black-crusted sheep's cheese – this makes a wonderful outdoor lunch in early summer.

The Tuscans are renowned throughout Italy for their love of beans; this has earned them the name of *mangiafagioli*, or 'bean-eaters'.

Early broad beans are among their favourite vegetables. They need hardly any cooking, and are tender and sweet when eaten raw. As the season progresses, the beans can be lightly cooked and, when cooled, pressed with thumb and forefinger from their almost translucent inner skins. Pushed through a sieve, they can be blended with Ricotta cheese to make an unusual and delicate stuffing for artichokes.

A traditional manner of cooking beans is *Fagioli al Fiasco* – beans in a flask with olive oil and garlic. The flask is stoppered and laid overnight in the coolest part of the dying fire, so that the beans cook very slowly and none of their aroma is lost.

The region also boasts that substantial appetizer, *Tonno e Fagioli,* beans with tuna fish, as well as all manner of bean soups and variations on a theme of beans using rice and pasta.

Spinach, a grim punishment for schoolchildren in northern lands, is another Tuscan delicacy. It is cooked for a short time in the water clinging to the leaves after washing, and thereby retains its bright emerald green colour before being thoroughly drained, then tossed in butter with a clove of garlic. Cooked in this way it has become so associated with Florence in the minds of foreign visitors, that abroad, the term *alla fiorentina,* nearly always means 'cooked with spinach'.

To the Italians, *alla fiorentina* is synonymous with Florence, not with spinach. *Bistecca alla Fiorentina* is perhaps the most famous example of Florentine cooking at its purest. T-bone steaks from two-year-old Chiana Valley bulls are cooked briefly over the fierce heat of a fragrant chestnut wood fire, then rubbed with salt, pepper and the finest olive oil.

This simple dish, which demands absolute perfection from its ingredients and the minimum of fuss but the maximum of dedication from its cook, is typical of Tuscan cooking. The freshest vegetables in their prime, the ripest juiciest fruit, newly picked from the garden or carefully selected from the market, the tenderest meat, the meatiest sausage – all are cooked with the utmost care, but simply, so that their flavours are allowed to shine through.

This is the very opposite of French cooking, with its subtle saucing and complicated symphonies of flavour – and it looks different too. In France, presented with a masterpiece of the culinary arts, you might not be able to tell at first glance what is on your plate. In Tuscany, there is no doubt. The bold bright colours – red peppers, purple aubergines, crackly brown meat – leap up at you. It is purely a matter of taste, and the Tuscans like their tastes pure.

In fact, French cooking owes a lot to Tuscany, and to Florence in particular – a debt acknowledged even in the bible of French cooking, the *Larousse Gastronomique*. In 1533, when French cooking was still in the Dark Ages, Catherine de Medici married the Dauphin, later Henri II of France. She took with her to France her own fleet of chefs and pastry cooks, and introduced the Florentine way of eating to her new homeland, along with vegetables the French had not tried before, among them broccoli, artichokes, haricot beans, savoy cabbage and petits pois. The French were quick to learn, and rapidly claimed the gastronomic arts for themselves.

And finally, wine. Wherever you go in Italy, you will be offered the wine of the region to drink with your meal. In Tuscany, this is Chianti.

It is said that Baron Bettino Ricasoli 'invented' Chianti in the 1860s. One night at a ball, his young wife was being paid too much attention for the Baron's liking. He called her away from her dancing partner and, together, they got into his carriage and drove all night, shivering in their finery, until they got to the castle of Brolio, a forbidding and gloomy ancestral home of the Baron's situated in the depths of the country well away from the temptations of dancing partners.

Here the couple made their home and, to pass the time, the Baron developed a new wine. He used a mixture of black Sangiovese and white Malavasia grapes, and devised a method of making them ferment twice, thereby giving the full red wine a novel taste and a slight tingle.

Chianti is today produced and exported on a large scale, but Chianti classico comes only from the area between Florence and Siena and bears the grower's label of a black cockerel against a gold background.

When the first fermentation is over, the must of dried grapes is added to the wine and a short second fermentation begins. Chianti made in this way is sold in the typical basket-covered flasks to be drunk young. The finer Chiantis are aged in the bottle. They are not fermented twice and are bottled in straight-sided claret bottles rather than in flasks.

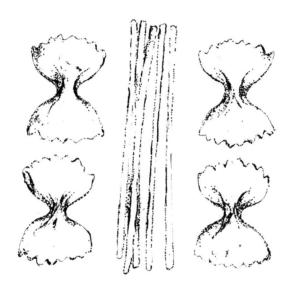

ANTIPASTI

Antipasti are most commonly a selection of savoury morsels such as slices of salami or *prosciutto*, or artichoke hearts, olives or little fish in oil or vinegar.

The idea of antipasti is to whet the appetite but not to drown it. It must be said, however, that Italian appetites are hearty and that this course of the meal, especially on feast days, when it is most frequently served, can reach gargantuan proportions.

In Tuscany raw broad beans and wafer-thin slices of fennel make a good summer appetizer together with a piece of salty *pecorino*, the local sheep's cheese. Another favourite is *Crostini alla Fiorentina;* these are slices of toasted bread topped with a savoury chicken liver pâté.

Olive all' Aglio
Garlic Olives

In Tuscany, fresh olives are harvested and treated in this way by the bucketful – the same method can be employed on a small scale to pep up a jar of shop-bought olives. Offer these olives with a drink before lunch or use them in any recipe where olives are required.

100g/4 oz olives in brine, drained
1 clove of garlic, crushed

1 sprig of rosemary
olive oil

Put the olives in a jar, add the garlic and rosemary, and cover with olive oil. Seal the jar, and leave for at least a week before using.

Note When all the olives have been eaten, use the garlicky olive oil to cook meat or as part of a salad dressing.

A Selection of Antipasti
Olive all' Aglio, Melone al Vino Bianco (page 15) and *Tonno e Fagioli (page 18)*

Pomodori al Fontina
Tomatoes with Fontina Cheese

This is a good way of using up leftover cooked rice or risotto.

4 Mediterranean tomatoes
salt, freshly ground black pepper
4 slices Fontina cheese

STUFFING
25g/1 oz butter (approx)
50g/2 oz mushrooms, chopped
100g/4 oz cooked rice or risotto (page 42 – 43)
2 slices Italian salami, chopped
a small handful of parsley, chopped

Cut the tops off the tomatoes, and scoop out the seeds and juice. Sprinkle the
insides with salt, and leave them upside-down to drain while
preparing the stuffing.
Melt the butter in a pan, and cook the mushrooms until black and juicy. Mix
with the cooked rice or risotto, the salami and parsley, and season to taste.
Fill the tomatoes with the stuffing, and arrange them in a buttered ovenproof
dish. Cook in a hot oven, 220°C/425°F/Gas 7, for about 10 minutes until
almost done, then top each tomato with a slice of Fontina cheese, and return
to the oven for about 5 minutes until bubbling and golden. Serve at once.

Funghi Ripieni
Stuffed Mushrooms

2 × 15ml spoons/2 tablespoons olive oil
8 large field mushrooms, stalks removed and
 finely chopped
1 onion, chopped
2 cloves garlic, crushed
2 × 15ml spoons/2 tablespoons chopped
 parsley

1 slice of stale bread, soaked, squeezed dry
 and crumbled
salt, freshly ground black pepper
1 egg, beaten
butter

Heat the oil in a pan, and gently cook the mushroom stalks, onion and garlic until soft, stirring occasionally. Remove from the heat, transfer to a bowl, and mix with the parsley, bread, seasoning and beaten egg.
Use this mixture to stuff the mushrooms. Put them in a buttered ovenproof dish, dot with butter, and bake in a fairly hot oven, 200°C/400°F/Gas 6, for 20 minutes until soft. Serve immediately.

Melone al Vino Bianco
Melon with White Wine

The melons should be ripe but not squashy. A ripe melon will sound hollow when flicked with your finger, and it will smell sweet and golden.

2 Cantaloupe melons
300ml/½ pint dry white wine
2 × 15ml spoons/2 tablespoons Marsala

DECORATION
sprigs borage or mint

Cut the melons in half crossways. Carefully spoon out the seeds and pith, then scoop the flesh into balls with a melon ball scoop. Put the balls in a bowl, then pour over the wine and Marsala, and leave to marinate for about 1 hour. Chill the melon shells at the same time.
Fill the shells with the melon balls, pour over the marinade and decorate with sprigs of borage or mint.

Crostini alla Fiorentina
Florentine-style Chicken Livers

25g/1 oz butter
1 × 15ml spoon/1 tablespoon olive oil
1 clove of garlic, crushed
1 small onion, minced
225g/8 oz chicken livers, finely chopped

a few leaves sage, chopped
2 anchovy fillets, soaked, drained and
  chopped
4 slices Italian bread, toasted

Heat together the butter and oil in a heavy-based pan, and gently cook the garlic and onion until golden, stirring occasionally. Add the chicken livers, sage and anchovy fillets, and continue to cook, stirring, for a few minutes until the livers can be crushed under the back of the spoon. Remove from the heat, mash with the spoon, spread on the toasted bread, and serve immediately.

Trippa alla Senese
Siennese Tripe with Vegetables

450g/1 lb tripe
50g/2 oz butter
2 × 15ml spoons/2 tablespoons olive oil
1 onion, chopped
1 clove of garlic, crushed
1 stick of celery, chopped

1 carrot, finely sliced
400g/14 oz canned tomatoes, drained and
  mashed, juice reserved
a pinch of cinnamon
a small pinch of paprika
salt, freshly ground black pepper

Put the tripe in a saucepan, cover with water, and bring to the boil. Cook, covered, for 15 minutes until tender, then drain and leave to cool. Cut into manageable pieces.
Meanwhile, heat the butter and olive oil in a pan, and gently cook the onion, garlic, celery and carrot until soft, stirring occasionally.
Add the tripe and tomatoes, and stir in the cinnamon, paprika, salt and pepper. Add the reserved tomato juice, if required, then heat through.
Divide the tripe between 4 individual heated dishes, and serve hot with grated Parmesan cheese and crusty Italian bread.

Crostini alla Fiorentina

Tonno e Fagioli
Tuna Fish with Beans

This substantial country starter can also make a quick lunch for two.

200g/7 oz canned tuna fish in oil, drained and
mashed
400g/14 oz canned beans (kidney, cannellini
or butter beans), drained
1 onion, finely chopped

a handful of parsley, chopped
salt, freshly ground black pepper
olive oil (optional)
wine vinegar or lemon juice (optional)

Mix together the ingredients and season well. Add a little olive oil and wine
vinegar or lemon juice, if liked.
Serve with crusty bread.

Insalata di Patate e Cipolle col Tonno
Potato, Onion and Tuna Fish Salad

4 medium-sized potatoes
200g/7 oz canned tuna fish, drained and
mashed
1 onion, chopped
1 × 15ml spoon/1 tablespoon capers

a handful of parsley, chopped
1 × 15ml spoon/1 tablespoon olive oil
a squeeze of lemon juice
salt, freshly ground black pepper

Boil the potatoes in their skins until tender, then drain and leave until cool
enough to handle. Peel, then cut into thick slices.
Toss the potato slices in a bowl with the tuna, onion, capers and parsley.
Pour over the olive oil and lemon juice, season to taste, and toss again. Serve
in small individual serving bowls while the potatoes are still warm.

Insalata di Polpette
Squid Salad

450g/1 lb squid
a few drops vinegar
2 × 15ml spoons/2 tablespoons olive oil
a squeeze of lemon juice
salt, freshly ground black pepper

1 clove of garlic, crushed
1 small red pepper, de-seeded and sliced
1 small yellow pepper, de-seeded and sliced
GARNISH
a few leaves basil, chopped

To prepare the squid, remove and discard the external membrane, the eyes, the cuttlefish bone and the ink sac. Put the squid in a pan of water with a few drops of vinegar, bring to the boil, then reduce the heat and simmer for about 30 minutes until tender. Drain well, then thinly slice.
Mix together the oil, lemon juice, seasoning and garlic.
Toss the squid and peppers in the dressing, and serve in small individual salad bowls, garnished with the basil.

Sardine al Forno
Baked Sardines

8 fresh sardines, cleaned and heads removed
salt, freshly ground black pepper
4 × 15ml spoons/4 tablespoons olive oil

a sprig of rosemary
1 clove of garlic, crushed
100g/4 oz breadcrumbs (approx)

Put the sardines in one layer in an ovenproof dish, season with salt and pepper, and pour over the olive oil. Break up the sprig of rosemary and tuck it between the fish, together with the garlic, if using. Leave to marinate for about 1 hour.
Remove the sardines with a slotted spoon, and roll them in breadcrumbs. Return to the dish, coat in the oil, and bake in a fairly hot oven, 200°C/400°F/ Gas 6, for 15 minutes until cooked through. Serve hot.

SOUPS & SAUCES

Soups in Italy are never followed by rice or pasta because they often contain rice and pasta themselves, and can replace a main course.

The basis of a good soup is a good stock or broth (*brodo*). This may be served quite plainly, with a few little dumplings or gnocchi or garnished with *crostini*.

A *minestrone* usually contains shredded vegetables such as carrot and cabbage, and in Tuscany you are unlikely to find a *minestrone* that does not have beans as one of its main ingredients. At the bottom of the soup bowl there will often be a slice of bread that has been toasted and rubbed with a clove of garlic.

Unless the soup has fish in it, such as the *Cacciucco* from Livorno, it will be served with a generous amount of Parmesan cheese. Some can be stirred into the soup when it has finished cooking, to thicken it, and more sprinkled on top at the table. In Tuscany, a dribble of the best gold green olive oil is often added to the soup at the last minute.

Serve your Italian soups in deep wide soup plates – some of the good things they contain are too big for more delicate dishes.

Zuppa di Fave
Broad Bean Soup

2 × 15ml spoons/2 tablespoons olive oil
1 onion, finely chopped
1 clove of garlic, finely chopped
3 leaves sage
50g/2 oz pancetta (bacon), diced

1.12kg/2½ lb broad beans, shelled
1.5 litres/2½ pints Brodo di Pollo (page 30)
salt, freshly ground black pepper
Parmesan cheese, grated

Heat the oil in a pan and gently cook the onion, garlic and sage until soft, stirring occasionally. Add the *pancetta* and beans, and pour the stock over. Season to taste, then cook slowly, covered, for about 10 minutes until the beans are tender.
Pour the soup through a sieve or colander. When the beans have cooled a little, slip them from their inner skins. Discard the skins and the sage, return the vegetables and *pancetta* to the soup, heat through, and serve immediately, sprinkled with Parmesan cheese.

Minestra di Pasta e Fagioli
Pasta and Bean Soup

Cannellini beans are also called *toscanelli* in recognition of the Tuscans' love of beans.

4 × 15ml spoons/4 tablespoons olive oil
1 onion, chopped
2 cloves garlic, chopped
225g/8 oz ripe tomatoes, skinned and
   chopped
a few sage leaves

1.2 litres/2 pints stock
150g/5 oz cooked cannellini beans
salt, freshly ground black pepper
150g/5 oz conchigliette (small pasta shells)
Parmesan cheese, grated

Heat the oil in a pan, and gently cook the onion and garlic until soft but not brown, stirring occasionally. Add the tomatoes and sage, and pour in the stock.
Purée half the beans in a blender or pass through a sieve, then add to the soup. Cover and cook gently for 18 minutes then add the remaining beans, season to taste, and add the pasta. Cook for a further 12 minutes. Serve immediately, sprinkled with Parmesan cheese.

Minestrone alla Livornese
Livorno-style Minestrone

350g/12 oz dried white beans, soaked
   overnight
3.6 litres/6 pints water
2 × 15ml spoons/2 tablespoons olive oil
1 clove of garlic, finely chopped
1 onion, finely chopped
1 stick of celery, finely chopped
1 carrot, finely chopped

1 × 15ml spoon/1 tablespoon concentrated
   tomato purée
1 courgette, diced
½ white cabbage, shredded or 450g/1 lb
   spinach, cooked and chopped
1 bunch of parsley, chopped
salt, freshly ground black pepper
4 slices Italian bread
Parmesan cheese, grated

Drain the beans, discarding the water, then boil them vigorously in the fresh water for 10 minutes. Reduce the heat, then cook slowly for about 1 hour until very tender.

Meanwhile, heat the oil in a pan, and gently cook the garlic, onion, celery and carrot until soft, stirring occasionally. Dilute the tomato purée with a little water, then stir into the pan.

Add the courgette, cabbage or spinach, the parsley and the cooked beans with their liquor. Season to taste, then cover and cook slowly for 20 minutes.

Lay a slice of bread in each soup bowl and ladle the soup on top. Serve immediately, sprinkled with Parmesan cheese.

Acquacotta
Wild Mushroom Soup

The name of this famous Tuscan soup means 'cooked water', signifying that it costs absolutely nothing to make. This is true if you know where to pick *porcini*. Otherwise you will have to buy them dried in an Italian delicatessen.

4 × 15ml spoons/4 tablespoons olive oil
2 cloves garlic, chopped
1 sprig of mint
salt, freshly ground black pepper
275g/10 oz fresh or dried porcini (ceps), cut
  into pieces (see **Note**)

½ sweet red pepper, chopped
1.2 litres/2 pints Brodo di Pollo (page 30)
4 eggs
4 × 15ml spoons/4 tablespoons grated
  Parmesan cheese
4 slices Italian crusty bread

Heat the olive oil in a pan, add the garlic and mint leaves and a little pepper. Let the garlic soften without browning. Add the *porcini* and chopped pepper, then turn down the heat to very low to allow them to give up their juices.
Season with salt, and pour the stock over. Cover the pan and simmer for 20 minutes.
Meanwhile, beat the eggs and cheese in a soup tureen.
Pour the soup over, and leave to stand, covered, for a few minutes while the soup cooks the eggs.
Lay a slice of bread in each soup bowl, and ladle the soup on top. Serve immediately.

Note If using dried *porcini* for this recipe, they should be soaked in water until plump, then drained and chopped.

Pappa col Pomodoro
Thrifty Tomato Soup

This is a Tuscan favourite, especially with children – a homely tomato soup made with the last slices of the loaf.

800g/1¾ lb ripe tomatoes, skinned, de-seeded and chopped
225g/8 oz white crusty bread, torn or crumbled
a handful of basil and sage leaves, mixed

4 cloves garlic, bruised
3 × 15ml spoons/3 tablespoons olive oil
1.2 litres/2 pints stock
salt, freshly ground black pepper

Put the tomatoes in a heavy-based saucepan with the bread, herbs and garlic. Heat gently, stirring constantly, until the bread and tomatoes form a thick 'pap', then add the olive oil. Pour the stock over, and season to taste. Cook gently for about 20 minutes, stirring occasionally, then serve.

Minestra di Lenticche e Pasta
Lentil Soup with Pasta

1 × 15ml spoon/1 tablespoon olive oil
1 onion, chopped
175g/6 oz brown lentils, soaked overnight and drained
1.2 litres/2 pints water (approx)

1 stock cube
salt, freshly ground black pepper
50g/2 oz anellini (ring-shaped pasta)
Parmesan cheese, grated

Heat the olive oil in a large saucepan, and gently cook the onion until soft, stirring occasionally. Add the lentils and water, bring to the boil, then crumble in the stock cube. Cook for about 1 hour until the lentils are tender, adding extra water if necessary.

Purée half the soup in a blender or pass through a sieve, then return to the pan, and season to taste. Add the pasta, and cook for a further 5 minutes until *al dente.* Serve hot, sprinkled with Parmesan cheese.

Pappa col Pomodoro

Zuppa di Ceci
Chick-pea Soup

2 × 15ml spoons/2 tablespoons olive oil
1 onion, finely chopped
1 clove of garlic, crushed
50g/2 oz prosciutto (Italian raw ham),
    chopped
100g/4 oz sieved tomatoes

a small handful of parsley, chopped
450g/1 lb cooked chick-peas
1.2 litres/2 pints Brodo di Pollo (page 30)
salt, freshly ground black pepper
4 slices Italian bread, toasted
Parmesan cheese, grated

Heat the oil in a pan, and gently cook the onion and garlic until soft, stirring
occasionally. Add the *prosciutto*, tomatoes, parsley and chick-peas. Pour the
stock over and cook gently for 30 minutes. Season to taste.
Lay a slice of toasted bread in each soup bowl, and ladle the soup on top.
Serve immediately, sprinkled with Parmesan cheese.

Zuppa di Castagne
Chestnut Soup

450g/1 lb chestnuts or 400g/14 oz canned
    chestnut purée
25g/1 oz butter
1 large onion, chopped
1 carrot, chopped

1 stick of celery, chopped
1.2 litres/2 pints Brodo di Pollo (page 30) or
    half milk, half stock
salt, freshly ground black pepper
crostini (page 9)

Pierce the chestnuts, if using, with a sharp knife, and boil for 20 minutes or
bake in a warm oven, 160°C/325°F/Gas 3, for 15 minutes. Remove the shells,
then peel away the inner skins.
Melt the butter in a large pan, and gently cook the onion, carrot and celery
until soft, stirring occasionally. Add the chestnuts or chestnut purée, pour
the stock over, and season to taste. Cover and cook until the chestnuts are
very tender.
Purée the soup in a blender or pass through a sieve, then return
to the pan to heat through.
Serve with *crostini*.

Brodo di Gallina con Gnocchetti di Fegato
Chicken Soup with Liver Dumplings

25g/1 oz butter
1 onion, finely chopped
200g/7 oz chicken livers
2 × 15ml spoons/2 tablespoons Marsala
a small handful of chopped parsley

50g/2 oz flour plus extra for coating
25g/1 oz Parmesan cheese, grated plus extra
  for serving
salt, freshly ground black pepper
1.2 litres/2 pints Brodo di Pollo (page 30)

Melt the butter in a pan, and gently cook the onion until soft, stirring occasionally. Add the livers and Marsala, and cook briskly until the livers have browned on all sides and the Marsala has evaporated.
Tip the mixture into a bowl, add the parsley, flour, Parmesan cheese and seasoning and mash until thoroughly combined. Divide the mixture into balls the size of walnuts, and roll them in flour, tapping off the excess.
Meanwhile, bring the chicken stock to the boil.
Add the dumplings to the stock, cook for 3–5 minutes, and serve immediately with extra Parmesan cheese.

Stracciatella

This famous soup came originally from Rome, but is now very popular in Tuscany. Its name means 'little rags'; this refers to the appearance of the flakes of cooked egg in the broth.

1.2 litres/2 pints stock
2 eggs
4 × 15ml spoons/4 tablespoons fine white
  breadcrumbs

4 × 15ml spoons/4 tablespoons grated
  Parmesan cheese
salt, freshly ground black pepper

Reserving about a cupful of stock, put the rest in a large pan, and bring to the boil.
Beat together the eggs with the breadcrumbs and Parmesan cheese, and season with a little salt and pepper. Add the reserved stock, and whisk well. Gradually pour the egg mixture into the boiling stock, stirring constantly. Reduce the heat and continue to cook, still stirring, for 2–3 minutes. By this time the egg will have cooked, forming the 'little rags'. Serve immediately.

Cacciucco
Fish Soup

Serves 4–8

This delicious fish soup is a speciality of Livorno and is substantial enough to be a meal in itself. Vary the ingredients according to availability.

4 × 15ml spoons/4 tablespoons olive oil
3 cloves garlic, chopped
1 hot red pepper, finely chopped
1 onion, chopped
1 stick of celery, chopped
225g/8 oz canned tomatoes
a handful of chopped parsley
salt, freshly ground black pepper

675g/1½ lb mixed octopus, squid, prawns, shrimps, langoustine, etc, cut into manageable pieces
150ml/¼ pint dry white wine
900g/2 lb mixed white fish (cod, hake, whiting, halibut, etc), cut into manageable pieces
4–8 slices stale Italian bread, toasted and rubbed with a cut clove of garlic

Heat the oil in a large pan, and cook the garlic and pepper until lightly browned, stirring occasionally. Add the onion and celery, and cook gently until soft, stirring occasionally. Add the tomatoes and parsley, season to taste and continue to cook, covered, for about 5 minutes. Add the squid, prawns etc, then pour over the wine. Cover, then cook for 30 minutes or until the squid is tender. Add the remaining fish and about 3 cups of water, then cook for a further 15 minutes until all the fish is cooked.

Lay a slice of toasted garlic bread in each soup bowl and ladle the soup on top. Serve immediately.

Cacciucco

Brodo di Manzo
Beef Stock

1.35kg/3 lb beef or veal bones
2 onions, roughly chopped
2 carrots, roughly chopped
2 sticks celery, roughly chopped

a bunch of parsley
salt
3 litres/5 pints water

Put the bones in a very large heavy pan over low heat for about 15 minutes, moving them about occasionally with a wooden spoon. Enough fat should come out of the marrow to fry them gently. Add the onions, carrots and celery, and stir until lightly browned. Add the parsley and a pinch of salt, and pour on the water. Bring the stock slowly to the boil, skimming occasionally. Half cover the pan, lower the heat, then simmer for about 3–4 hours. Strain the stock, and use as required.

Brodo di Pollo
Chicken Stock

You can use all the chicken giblets to make this stock apart from the liver, which will overpower the delicate flavour with bitterness.

chicken giblets, minus the liver
chicken bones, if available
1 onion, roughly chopped
1 bay leaf

1 sprig of thyme
3 stalks parsley
1.2 litres/2 pints water
a pinch of salt

Put all the ingredients in a large pan, and simmer gently, half covered, for about 1 hour, skimming occasionally. Strain the stock, and use as required.

Salsa Besciamella
Béchamel Sauce

Makes 300ml/½ pint (approx)

40g/1½ oz butter
40g/1½ oz flour
300ml/½ pint milk
75g/3 oz grated hard cheese, preferably
  Parmesan

salt, freshly ground black pepper
1–2 egg yolks (optional)
a pinch of nutmeg (optional)

Melt the butter in a small, heavy-based pan over moderate heat; do not allow
it to brown. Remove from the heat, and stir in the flour. Return to gentle
heat, and add the milk gradually, stirring all the time. Raise the heat slightly
as the sauce thickens and let it bubble; stir constantly. Add the cheese, and
stir until it has melted. Season well.
Remove the sauce from the heat, leave to cool a little, then add the egg yolks
and nutmeg if a richer sauce is required.

Ragù
Meat and Tomato Sauce

Makes 900ml/1½ pints (approx)

Ragù is one of the staples of a pasta cook's kitchen. Use it with spaghetti, gnocchi or
polenta, or in layers with *Salsa Besciamella* in a baked lasagne.

2 × 15ml spoons/2 tablespoons olive oil
1 onion, chopped
1 stick of celery, chopped
1 carrot, chopped
1 × 15ml spoon/1 tablespoon chopped parsley
225g/8 oz lean minced beef

50g/2 oz prosciutto (raw Italian ham) or
  pancetta (bacon), chopped
400g/14 oz tomatoes, skinned and chopped or
  canned tomatoes, drained
salt, freshly ground black pepper

Heat the olive oil in a pan, and gently cook the onion, celery and carrot until
soft, stirring occasionally. Add the parsley and minced beef and cook until
the beef turns pink. Add the remaining ingredients, then simmer for about 30
minutes, stirring occasionally. Season to taste. Serve hot.

Salsa Verde
Green Sauce

Makes 100ml/4 fl oz (approx)

1 clove of garlic, crushed
2 anchovy fillets, soaked, drained and
* chopped*
1 × 15ml spoon/1 tablespoon capers, chopped
1 × 15ml spoon/1 tablespoon chopped parsley

1 small potato, boiled and mashed
black pepper
1 × 15ml spoon/1 tablespoon wine vinegar
3 × 15ml spoons/3 tablespoons olive oil

Mix together the garlic, anchovy fillets, capers, parsley and mashed potato, then season with black pepper. Mix the vinegar with the oil and pour this gradually on to the sauce, stirring all the time.
Pour the sauce over cold chicken or poached white fish, and serve with lemon wedges.

Salsa di Pomodoro
Tomato Sauce

Makes 300ml/½ pint (approx)

2 × 15ml spoons/2 tablespoons olive oil
1 onion, chopped
1–2 cloves garlic, chopped
1 stick of celery, chopped
1 carrot, grated
400g/14 oz canned tomatoes, drained and
* juice reserved*

2 × 15ml spoons/2 tablespoons concentrated
* tomato purée*
a few freshly chopped herbs (sage, basil,
* parsley, thyme, according to taste)*
salt, freshly ground black pepper

Heat the oil in a pan, and gently cook the onion, garlic, celery and carrot until soft, stirring occasionally. Add the tomatoes, mashing them up as you do so. Reserve the juice for thinning down the sauce, if required. Stir in the tomato purée and herbs, and season well. Simmer until the sauce has thickened. Use it as it is, or purée until smooth.

A Selection of Sauces
Salsa Verde, Ragù (page 31) and Salsa di Pomodoro

PASTA, RICE, GNOCCHI & POLENTA

Pasta is usually the main lunch-time dish in a Tuscan household. It may be served very simply with olive oil, garlic and Parmesan cheese or with a *Ragù* or other sauce, often containing beans.

Rice is, however, often cooked in the same pot with the meat, fish or vegetables whereas gnocchi and polenta, though they can be baked with a sauce, are often served separately as an accompaniment, instead of bread or potatoes.

The texture of an Italian risotto is very different to that of an Indian pullao. The Italians do not aim for dry fluffy rice. Though the grains should be separate and still *al dente*, they should be moist, absorbing the flavours of the thick sauce in which they are cooked.

Fusilli alla Panna con Porcini
Pasta Twists with Cream and Ceps

400g/14 oz fusilli *(pasta twists)*
1 × 15ml spoon/1 tablespoon olive oil
salt, freshly ground black pepper
150ml/¼ pint single cream

50g/2 oz dried porcini *(ceps), soaked, drained and chopped*
25g/1 oz butter
50g/2 oz Parmesan cheese, grated

Cook the pasta in a large pan of steadily boiling water until *al dente* with the olive oil and 1 × 5ml spoon/1 teaspoon salt.
Meanwhile, warm the cream in a double saucepan together with the *porcini*.
In a separate pan, melt the butter over low heat, and stir in the Parmesan cheese.
Drain the pasta thoroughly, and transfer to a heated tureen. Pour over the cream and butter sauces, toss well, season with black pepper, and serve immediately.

34

Tagliatelle Paglia e Fieno
Tagliatelle 'Straw and Hay'

This recipe is so called because of the mixture of yellow and green pasta.

2 × 15ml spoons/2 tablespoons olive oil
25g/1 oz butter
1 small onion, chopped
1 carrot, chopped
1 stick of celery, chopped
200g/7 oz lean minced beef
50g/2 oz pancetta (bacon), chopped
150ml/¼ pint red wine
25g/1 oz dried porcini (ceps), soaked, drained and finely chopped

1 × 15ml spoon/1 tablespoon concentrated tomato purée
salt, freshly ground black pepper
1 bay leaf
1 clove of garlic, finely chopped
3 chicken livers, chopped
200g/7 oz egg tagliatelle
200g/7 oz spinach tagliatelle
Parmesan cheese, grated

Heat together 1 × 15ml spoon/1 tablespoon oil and the butter in a pan, and gently cook the onion, carrot and celery until softened but not brown, stirring occasionally.

In a separate pan, cook the minced beef over low heat until all the fat runs out; stir occasionally. Drain well, then add to the vegetables. Stir in the *pancetta* and pour the wine over. Cook until this has evaporated, then add the *porcini* and tomato purée, diluted with a little water. Season with salt, add the bay leaf and garlic, and cook, covered, over low heat for about 30 minutes until the meat is done, adding a little water to prevent the sauce from drying out if necessary. About 5 minutes before the end of the cooking time, add the chicken livers to the sauce.

Meanwhile, cook the pasta in a large pan of steadily boiling water until *al dente* with the remaining oil and 1 × 5ml spoon/1 teaspoon salt.

Drain the pasta thoroughly, transfer to a heated serving dish, and sprinkle with pepper and Parmesan cheese. Pour the sauce over, and serve immediately with more Parmesan cheese.

Penne con Prosciutto e Piselli
Penne with Prosciutto and Peas

Penna means 'feather' in Italian – a feather is a quill, and a quill is a pen.

400g/14 oz penne (nib-shaped pasta)
1 × 15ml spoon/1 tablespoon olive oil
salt, freshly ground black pepper
50g/2 oz butter

100g/4 oz lean prosciutto (Italian raw ham),
  cut into strips
100g/4 oz cooked fresh peas
150ml/¼ pint double cream
Parmesan cheese, grated

Cook the pasta in a large pan of steadily boiling water until *al dente* with the
olive oil and 1 × 5ml spoon/1 teaspoon salt.
Meanwhile, melt the butter in a pan, and gently cook the *prosciutto* and peas
for about 5 minutes to heat through, stirring occasionally.
Warm the cream gently in a double boiler.
Drain the pasta thoroughly, and transfer to a heated tureen. Stir in the
prosciutto and peas, sprinkle with the Parmesan cheese, pour over the cream,
toss well, and season with black pepper. Serve immediately.

Conchiglie al Gorgonzola
Pasta Shells with Gorgonzola Cream Sauce

The sauce for this pasta recipe takes very few minutes to prepare. Serve with a crisp
radicchio salad for a sharp contrast in flavour and colour.

400g/14 oz conchiglie (pasta shells)
1 × 15ml spoon/1 tablespoon olive oil
salt, freshly ground black pepper

100g/4 oz ripe Gorgonzola cheese
150ml/¼ pint double cream

Cook the pasta in a large pan of steadily boiling water until *al dente* with the
olive oil and 1 × 5ml spoon/1 teaspoon salt.
Meanwhile, mix the Gorgonzola and cream in a blender or pound in a bowl
with a wooden spoon. Heat through in a double boiler.
Drain the pasta thoroughly, transfer to a heated tureen, and sprinkle liberally
with black pepper. Pour the sauce over, toss well
and serve immediately.

Penne con Prosciutto e Piselli

Lasagne ai Funghi
Mushroom Lasagne

75g/3 oz butter
3 × 15ml spoons/3 tablespoons olive oil
1 small onion, finely chopped
275g/10 oz mushrooms, chopped
225g/8 oz canned tomatoes, drained and
  mashed, juice reserved

50g/2 oz pancetta *(bacon)*, chopped
salt, freshly ground black pepper
400g/14 oz lasagne
50g/2 oz Parmesan cheese, grated

Heat the butter and 2 × 15ml spoons/2 tablespoons oil in a deep frying pan, and gently cook the onion and mushrooms, stirring occasionally, until the mushrooms are very black and have given up their juices. Add the tomatoes and *pancetta*, season to taste, then cover and cook for about 30 minutes, adding a little of the reserved tomato juice if necessary to prevent the sauce from drying out.
Meanwhile, cook the pasta in a large pan of steadily boiling water until *al dente* with the remaining olive oil and 1 × 5ml spoon/1 teaspoon salt.
Drain the pasta thoroughly, then arrange in layers with the sauce in an oblong serving dish, sprinkling each layer of sauce with Parmesan cheese. Serve immediately.

Tuoni e Lampo
'Thunder and Lightning'

This curious name is given to a dish of pasta and *ceci* (chick-peas),

200g/7 oz dried chick-peas, soaked overnight,
  then drained
400g/14 oz farfalle *(bow-shaped pasta)*
1 × 15ml spoon/1 tablespoon olive oil

salt, freshly ground black pepper
40g/1½ oz butter
5 × 15ml spoons/5 tablespoons grated
  Parmesan cheese

Cook the chick-peas slowly for about 5 hours until tender, depending on their age.
Meanwhile, cook the pasta in a large pan of steadily boiling water until *al dente* with the olive oil and 1 × 5ml spoon/1 teaspoon salt.
Drain the pasta and chick-peas, and toss together in a heated tureen with the butter and Parmesan cheese. Season with salt and plenty of black pepper, and serve immediately.

Bucatini alla Marinara
Bucatini with Mussels

900g/2 lb mussels
4 × 15ml spoons/4 tablespoons dry white
  wine
a handful of parsley, chopped
4 × 15ml spoons/4 tablespoons olive oil
3 cloves garlic, crushed

350g/12 oz ripe tomatoes, skinned, de-seeded
  and chopped
a handful of basil leaves
salt, freshly ground black pepper
400g/14 oz bucatini (thin spaghetti)
paprika

Scrub the mussels well under cold running water, and scrape off the beards.
Discard any with broken shells. Put in a pan with the wine and parsley, cover
tightly and cook over low heat for about 7 minutes until the mussels open.
Discard any mussels that remain closed. Remove the mussels from their
shells, and put to one side. Reserve the cooking liquor.

Heat 3 × 15ml spoons/3 tablespoons olive oil in a large pan, and gently cook
the garlic until soft, stirring occasionally. Add the tomatoes, the mussel
cooking liquor and the basil, and season with salt and pepper. Cook gently
until soft, stirring occasionally.

Meanwhile, cook the *bucatini* in a large pan of steadily boiling water until *al
dente* with the remaining olive oil and 1 × 5ml spoon/1 teaspoon salt.

Just before the pasta is ready, add the mussels to the sauce with a very little
paprika.

Drain the pasta thoroughly, and transfer to a heated serving dish. Pour the
sauce over, and serve immediately.

Pasta con Intingolio di Fagioli
Pasta with Borlotti Bean Sauce

675g/1½ lb fresh borlotti beans, shelled
salt, freshly ground black pepper
5 × 15ml spoons/5 tablespoons olive oil
1 small onion, chopped
1 clove of garlic, crushed
450g/1 lb ripe tomatoes, skinned and
  de-seeded

50g/2 oz pancetta (bacon), chopped
a handful of parsley, chopped
a sprig of rosemary
400g/14 oz mafaldine (shaped tagliatelle)
Parmesan cheese, grated

Cook the borlotti beans in a pan of boiling salted water
until tender, then drain well.
Heat 4 × 15ml spoons/4 tablespoons oil in a pan, and gently cook the onion
and garlic until soft, stirring occasionally. Add the tomatoes, beans, *pancetta*,
herbs and seasoning, then cover and cook over low heat until the sauce is
thick and smooth, stirring occasionally and adding a little water if necessary
to prevent it sticking.
Meanwhile, cook the pasta in a large pan of steadily boiling water until *al
dente* with the remaining oil and 1 × 5ml spoon/1 teaspoon salt.
Drain the pasta thoroughly, and transfer to a heated serving dish. Pour the
sauce over, and serve immediately, sprinkled with Parmesan cheese.

Variation
Use dried cooked borlotti beans and canned tomatoes, if preferred.

Cannelloni Ripieni
Stuffed Cannelloni

50g/2 oz butter
3 × 15ml spoons/3 tablespoons olive oil
1 small onion, chopped
1 stalk of celery, chopped
1 carrot, grated
200g/7 oz lean minced veal
200g/7 oz lean minced beef
100g/4 oz prosciutto (raw Italian ham), chopped

150ml/¼ pint red wine
salt, freshly ground black pepper
1 bay leaf
2 × 15ml spoons/2 tablespoons concentrated tomato purée
350g/12 oz cannelloni
450ml/¾ pint Salsa Besciamella (page 31), using 2 additional egg yolks
Parmesan cheese, grated

Heat the butter and 2 × 15ml spoons/2 tablespoons olive oil in a large pan, and gently cook the vegetables until soft, stirring occasionally. Add the veal, beef and *prosciutto*, pour the wine over, season to taste, then add the bay leaf. Stir in the tomato purée, cover tightly and cook slowly for 45 minutes–1 hour, stirring occasionally and adding a little water or wine if the sauce shows any signs of drying out.

Meanwhile, cook the cannelloni in a large pan of steadily boiling water until almost *al dente* with the remaining olive oil and 1 × 5ml spoon/1 teaspoon salt. Refresh under cold running water, then drain thoroughly.

Stuff the cannelloni tubes with the meat mixture, discarding the bay leaf, and arrange in layers in a deep oblong ovenproof dish with the *Salsa Besciamella*. Finish with a layer of sauce, and sprinkle with the Parmesan cheese. Cook in a fairly hot oven, 200°C/400°F/Gas 6, for 15–20 minutes until golden-brown and bubbling. Serve immediately, accompanied by a green salad.

Risotto alla Toscana
Tuscan-style Risotto

A risotto should be moist and not dry. The grains of rice should be tender, yet with a bit of bite left in them.

2 × 15ml spoons/2 tablespoons olive oil
50g/2 oz butter
1 clove of garlic, chopped
1 onion, chopped
1 small carrot, chopped
1 stick of celery, chopped
225g/8 oz minced veal

100g/4 oz chicken livers
150ml/¼ pint red wine
450g/1 lb Italian rice
1.2 litres/2 pints boiling Brodo di Pollo *(page 30)*
2 × 15ml spoons/2 tablespoons grated Parmesan cheese

Heat together the oil and half the butter in a pan, then cook the garlic and onion until browned, stirring occasionally. Add the carrot, celery, veal, chicken livers and wine, and cook over moderate heat for about 5 minutes. Stir in the rice, coating it with the sauce, then cook for 8 minutes, stirring occasionally. Add the chicken stock, a ladleful at a time, until it has all been absorbed into the rice. Continue to cook over moderate heat until the rice is *al dente*. Remove from the heat, stir in the remaining butter and the Parmesan cheese, and serve immediately in hot soup plates.

Risotto con la Zucca
Rice with Pumpkin

75g/3 oz butter
450g/1 lb pumpkin flesh, diced
1.2 litres/2 pints boiling water (approx)

400g/14 oz Italian rice
2 chicken or vegetable stock cubes
4 × 15ml spoons/4 tablespoons grated Parmesan cheese

Melt half the butter in a pan, add the diced pumpkin, and cook gently for a few minutes. Add a ladle of boiling water, cover the pan and cook the pumpkin until it feels about half cooked. Stir in the rice, then crumble in the stock cubes. Start adding boiling water by the ladle, waiting until each addition has been absorbed before adding the rest. When the rice will absorb no more, continue to cook until *al dente*. Remove from the heat, stir in the remaining butter and the Parmesan cheese, and serve immediately in hot soup plates.

Risotto alla Paesana
Country-style Risotto

100g/4 oz butter
1 onion, chopped
1 carrot, chopped
1 stick of celery, chopped
1 leek, sliced (if available)
350g/12 oz Italian rice
450g/1 lb fresh borlotti beans, shelled or
    225g/8 oz canned borlotti beans

450g/1 lb fresh peas, shelled or 225g/8 oz
    canned peas
2 chicken or vegetable stock cubes
a few leaves sage
salt, freshly ground black pepper
4 × 15ml spoons/4 tablespoons grated
    Parmesan cheese

Melt half the butter in a pan, and gently cook the onion, carrot, celery and leek (if using) until soft, stirring occasionally. Stir in the rice, and coat with the mixture. Cook for a few minutes until translucent. Add the beans and peas, crumble in the stock cubes, then start adding boiling water by the ladle, waiting until each addition has been absorbed before adding the next. When the rice will absorb no more, add the sage and continue cooking until the rice is *al dente*. Season to taste, then stir in the remaining butter and the Parmesan cheese. Serve immediately in hot soup plates.

Gnocchi di Spinaci e Ricotta
Spinach and Ricotta Gnocchi

675g/1½ lb spinach, washed, stalks and
  discoloured leaves discarded
40g/1½ oz butter
salt, freshly ground black pepper
a pinch of nutmeg
225g/8 oz Ricotta cheese

50g/2 oz flour
1 egg, beaten
1–2 × 15ml spoons/1–2 tablespoons hot
  melted butter
Parmesan cheese, grated

Cram the spinach into a pan, cover and cook in the water clinging to the
leaves for about 8 minutes, stirring occasionally. Drain very well,
then chop finely.
Melt the butter in a pan, add the spinach, seasoning and nutmeg, and cook
until all the butter has been absorbed, stirring occasionally.
Sieve the Ricotta into a bowl, and mix well with the flour. Stir in the chopped
spinach and the egg, and mix thoroughly. Season to taste.
Shape the mixture with floured hands into balls the size of walnuts, and drop
them into a large pan of boiling salted water, a few at a time. As they rise to
the top, remove them with a slotted spoon. Transfer to a buttered ovenproof
dish, and keep hot. When the gnocchi are all ready, dribble over some hot
melted butter, sprinkle with Parmesan cheese,
and serve immediately.

Gnocchi di Spinaci e Ricotta

Polenta

Polenta is a very ancient dish and derives from the Roman *pulmentum*. It is a staple in Lombardy, Piedmont and Veneto, and is today also enjoyed further south in Tuscany. Made most often with yellow maize flour, it can be served thick, hot and porridge-like straight from the cooking pot, or it can be allowed to cool on a wooden surface, then cut like a cake and fried or baked with a sauce.
You will need a long-handled spoon for stirring so that you can keep as far away from the spitting boiling water as possible.

1.2 litres/2 pints water
salt
225g/8 oz polenta flour (yellow maize flour, chestnut flour or buckwheat flour)

100g/4 oz butter (optional)
100g/4 oz Parmesan cheese, grated (optional)

Bring the water to a full rolling boil in a large pan. Add a pinch of salt. Gradually pour in the flour, stirring all the time with a long-handled wooden spoon. If too much flour is added all at once, it will stick together and go lumpy. When all the flour has been added, the polenta should be thick and smooth. Cover the pan, lower the heat and cook for about 35 minutes, stirring occasionally until it resembles porridge. Loosen the polenta from the sides of the pan with a spatula. At this stage the butter can be mixed in together with the grated cheese. Season to taste, and serve the polenta as it is with *Salsa di Pomodoro* (page 32), or tip it out on to a board, shape it into a cake, and leave to cool.
When cool, the polenta can be sliced and served instead of bread or potatoes, or cooked again with a sauce, as in the recipes opposite.

Polenta ai Funghi
Polenta with Mushroom Sauce

1 recipe quantity polenta (page 46)
SAUCE
2 × 15ml spoons/2 tablespoons olive oil
25g/1 oz butter
225g/8 oz mushrooms, sliced

100g/4 oz prosciutto, (raw Italian ham)
  diced
about 400ml/⅔ pint Salsa di Pomodoro (page
  32)
4–6 × 15ml spoons/4–6 tablespoons grated
  Pecorino cheese

To prepare the sauce, heat together the olive oil and butter in a pan, and cook
the mushrooms until very black and tender. Add the *prosciutto*, then
stir in the sauce.
Cut the polenta into slabs, slices or rounds, and arrange them in a buttered
ovenproof dish in layers with the sauce, or simply pour the sauce over.
Sprinkle the Pecorino cheese on top, and cook in a hot oven, 220°C/425°F/
Gas 7, for about 10 minutes until golden-brown on top and hot through.
Serve at once.

Polenta Teneri alla Livornese
Livorno-style Polenta

1 recipe quantity polenta (page 46)
1 recipe quantity Ragù (page 31)

50g/2 oz Parmesan cheese, grated

Pour the polenta into four greased individual ovenproof dishes. Divide the
Ragù between the dishes, and top with the cheese. Bake in a fairly hot oven,
200°C/400°F/Gas 6, for 15 minutes until bubbling, and serve immediately,
with more Parmesan cheese, if liked.

FISH

Sea fish is rarely encountered in Tuscany – or anywhere else in Italy for that matter – except along the coast. Thus you can always be sure that it is absolutely fresh.

Favourite methods of cooking fish are the simple ones of frying and grilling rather that a profusion of garnishes and sauces. Serve with lemon wedges and a green salad. It is not usual to serve hot vegetables as accompaniments.

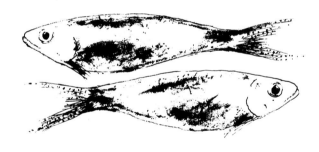

Trotelle al Burro e Salvia (page 51)

Baccalà in Umido
Stewed Salt Cod

Baccalà is sold in large drums in Italian delicatessens. Correctly prepared, it has a dense rather than a chewy texture.

900g/2 lb baccalà *(dried cod preserved in salt)*
4 × 15ml spoons/4 tablespoons olive oil
225g/8 oz whole baby onions, peeled
350g/12 oz potatoes, peeled and thinly sliced

400g/14 oz canned tomatoes, drained, juice
 reserved
2 × 15ml spoons/2 tablespoons concentrated
 tomato purée
salt, freshly ground black pepper

To soften the baccalà and get rid of the salt, soak for 24 hours in frequent changes of water or in a bowl under a gently running tap. Remove the skin, then cut the fish into equal-sized pieces.
Heat the olive oil in a flameproof casserole, and gently cook the onions until browned, stirring occasionally. Add the pieces of fish and the sliced potatoes. Mash the tomatoes with the tomato purée, then pour this over the fish. Season with salt and pepper, cover and cook over gentle heat for about 40 minutes until the fish and potatoes are tender and the sauce is thick; turn the fish pieces carefully two or three times and add a little of the reserved tomato juice if necessary.
Serve with slices of fried polenta (page 46) or Italian bread.

Aringhe alla Griglia
Grilled Herrings

4 herrings, cleaned and rinsed
olive oil
a sprig of rosemary (optional)

50g/2 oz butter
1 × 5ml spoon/1 teaspoon mustard powder
salt, freshly ground black pepper

Lay the herrings on a grill, and sprinkle with olive oil. Grill each side under a hot flame, basting occasionally with olive oil. Use a sprig of rosemary to paint the fish with oil or a pastry brush if no rosemary is to hand.
Meanwhile, melt the butter in a small pan, stir in the mustard, and season with salt and pepper.
Remove the fish from the grill, and arrange on a heated platter. Pour over the mustard sauce, and serve immediately, accompanied by crusty bread and a sharp-flavoured crisp salad.

Anguilla alla Fiorentina
Florentine-style Eels

4 × 15ml spoons/4 tablespoons olive oil
  (approx)
1 onion, finely chopped
1 clove of garlic, crushed
900g/2 lb eels, prepared by the fishmonger
  and cut into manageable pieces
flour

400g/14 oz canned peas, drained
400g/14 oz canned tomatoes, mashed, juice
  reserved
1 bay leaf
salt, freshly ground black pepper
a squeeze of lemon juice

Heat the oil in a flameproof casserole, and gently cook the onion and garlic until soft, stirring occasionally. Coat the pieces of eel in flour, and add to the casserole. Cook briskly until browned on all sides. Add the peas, the tomatoes and their juice and the bay leaf. Season well, then add a squeeze of lemon juice to taste. Cover the casserole, reduce the heat, and cook slowly for about 30 minutes, stirring occasionally.
Serve with mashed potato to mop up the juices, or in soup bowls with crusty bread.

Trotelle al Burro e Salvia
Trout with Sage

This is a very simple recipe enjoyed in the Tuscan hills and best made with freshly caught fish and sage picked on the way home from the trout stream. Let your imagination supply these ingredients should they be missing from your meal.

4 trout, cleaned and rinsed
seasoned flour
75g/3 oz butter
a few leaves sage

salt, freshly ground black pepper
GARNISH
lemon wedges

Roll the trout in seasoned flour. Melt the butter in a large heavy-based pan, and, when it begins to bubble, add the trout and sage. Cook gently for about 3 minutes on each side, according to size. Remove from the pan, season with salt and pepper, and serve immediately, garnished with lemon wedges.

Triglie alla Livornese
Livorno-style Mullet

4 mullet, cleaned and rinsed
seasoned flour
3 × 15ml spoons/3 tablespoons olive oil
1 small onion, finely chopped

1 clove of garlic, finely chopped
1 stick of celery, finely chopped
a handful of mixed basil and parsley, chopped
300ml/½ pint Salsa di Pomodoro (page 32)

Coat the mullet in seasoned flour. Heat the oil in a large heavy-based pan, and cook the mullet gently for 3 minutes on each side. Add the onion, garlic, celery and herbs, then pour over the sauce, and continue cooking for a further 3 minutes or until the sauce is hot. Serve immediately.

Triglie al Prosciutto
Mullet with Prosciutto

4 mullet, cleaned and rinsed
3 × 15ml spoons/3 tablespoons olive oil
3 × 15ml spoons/3 tablespoons lemon juice
salt, freshly ground black pepper

a few leaves sage
4 slices prosciutto (Italian raw ham)
GARNISH
lemon wedges

Put the mullet in one layer in an ovenproof dish, pour over the olive oil and lemon juice and sprinkle with salt and pepper. Add the sage leaves, then leave to marinate for about 1 hour.
Remove the fish with a slotted spoon, and wrap each one in a slice of prosciutto. Return to the dish, turn in the marinade, and bake in a fairly hot oven, 190°C/375°F/Gas 5, for 20 minutes until cooked through. Serve immediately, garnished with lemon wedges.

Triglie al Prosciutto

Carpa alle Olive
Carp with Olives

100g/4 oz green olives, stoned
2 or 3 anchovy fillets, soaked, drained and
  chopped
1 × 900g/2 lb carp
1 carrot, sliced
1 stick of celery, sliced

salt
1 × 5ml spoon/1 teaspoon white peppercorns
600ml/1 pint dry white wine (approx)
40g/1½ oz butter
40g/1½ oz flour

Stuff the olives with the chopped anchovy fillets. Put in a small pan, cover
with water, bring to the boil, then drain well.
Lay the carp in a fish kettle or a flameproof dish large enough to hold it in
one piece. Arrange the carrot, celery and olives around the fish. Add a pinch
of salt and the peppercorns, and pour the wine over. Cover the fish kettle or
dish, and poach over moderate heat for about 1 hour until tender.
When the fish is almost done, melt the butter in a small saucepan, then
stir in the flour until smooth.
Carefully transfer the fish to a large heated platter, and arrange the vegetables
and olives around it. Keep warm until ready to serve.
Add enough of the fish cooking liquor (minus the peppercorns) to the butter
and flour to make a smooth sauce. Serve as an
accompaniment to the fish.

Filetti di Sogliola in Carpione
Marinated Fillets of Sole

4 sole, filleted and skinned
25g/1 oz pine nut kernels
25g/1 oz sultanas, plumped up in boiling
  water and drained

1 large onion, chopped
150ml/¼ pint white wine vinegar (approx)
salt, freshly ground white pepper
1 bay leaf

Lay the fish in a large flat dish. Sprinkle with the pine nut kernels, the
sultanas and onion. Pour over the vinegar just to cover, then season with salt
and pepper, and tuck the bay leaf between the fish fillets. Cover the dish with
clingfilm, and leave to marinate for 2 days in a refrigerator.
Serve as a summer lunch, accompanied by a crisp salad.

Polpette al Pomodoro
Squid in a Tomato Sauce

675g/1½ lb squid
3 × 15ml spoons/3 tablespoons olive oil
1 clove of garlic, crushed
1 small onion, chopped

400g/14 oz canned tomatoes, mashed, juice
  reserved
a handful of basil leaves, chopped
salt, freshly ground black pepper
400g/14 oz Italian rice

To prepare the squid, remove and discard the external membrane, the eyes,
the cuttlefish bone and the ink sac. Slice the body and
the tentacles into rings.
Heat half the oil in a large frying pan, and gently cook the garlic and onion
until soft, stirring occasionally. Add the squid, tomatoes, basil and seasoning,
and cook gently for about 30 minutes, adding some of the reserved tomato
juice if necessary to prevent the fish from drying out.
Meanwhile, heat the remaining olive oil in a saucepan, add the rice, and stir
until well coated and translucent. Add boiling water by the ladle, waiting
until each addition has been absorbed before adding the next. Continue
cooking until the rice is *al dente*.
Spread the rice on a large heated platter, pile the squid and tomatoes on top,
and serve immediately.

MEAT

The Tuscans have always been great meat eaters, and claim that their Chiana Valley bulls give the best beef in the world – a claim that would no doubt be disputed by cattle farmers in other regions of Italy, who would be equally confident about the superiority of their own animals.

Beef is called *manzo;* veal is *vitello* or *vitella;* and there is also *vitellone,* which comes from a slightly older animal than *vitello,* but, nevertheless, an animal that has not been put to work. *Vitellone* is also the name given to young men who stand round idly on street corners!

Pork is perhaps preferred cured in the form of hams and sausages, but lamb is eaten with great relish, traditionally roasted with garlic, olive oil and rosemary and accompanied by a dish of broad beans.

The Tuscan cook is particularly inventive with offal. Cooked in wine with herbs and tomatoes, onions and garlic, it can be as delicious as any of the more expensive cuts of meat.

Fette di Filetto All' acciuga (page 58)

Fette di Filetto All'acciuga
Fillet Steak with Anchovy Butter

50g/2 oz butter
4 fillet steaks
ANCHOVY BUTTER
100g/4 oz butter, softened

2 × 15ml spoons/2 tablespoons anchovy paste
   (available in tubes)
freshly ground black pepper
GARNISH
4 anchovy fillets, soaked and drained

Make the anchovy butter first. Cream together the butter and anchovy paste in a small bowl, and season with pepper. Form into a fat sausage shape, wrap in foil, then chill for a couple of hours until hard.

Melt the 50g/2 oz butter in a pan large enough to hold the steak in one layer, and fry the meat briskly for about 5 minutes on each side. Transfer to a heated serving dish, and top each steak with a slice of anchovy butter and a rolled anchovy. Serve immediately.

Bistecca alla Fiorentina
Florentine-style Steak

A Florentine speciality, the sucess of this recipe depends on the quality of the meat. It is at its best when cooked over a fire of fragrant wood, such as chestnut. Failing this, use a very hot grill.

2 large T-bone steaks
olive oil

salt, freshly ground black pepper
lemon wedges

Put the steaks on the grill, and cook by a very hot flame for about 3 minutes until well cooked on the outside. Turn them over, using a spatula or tongs – avoid piercing them with a fork. Rub the cooked side with a little olive oil, and season with salt and pepper. Repeat on the other side. Cut each steak in two, and serve with lemon wedges.

Note The steaks should be well done on the outside and tender, pink and juicy in the centre. It is important not to season them before cooking, as this will toughen them. Some people like to rub them with a cut clove of garlic before grilling.

Agnello al Vino Bianco
Lamb in White Wine

900g/2 lb leg of lamb
1 clove of garlic
salt, freshly ground black pepper
2 × 15ml spoons/2 tablespoons olive oil
1 onion, sliced
2 large tomatoes, quartered

2 carrots, sliced
2 sticks celery, sliced
a few leaves sage
150ml/¼ pint dry white wine
juice of ½ orange

Rub the lamb with the cut clove of garlic, and sprinkle with salt and pepper. Heat the oil in a flameproof casserole, and gently cook the onion until golden, stirring occasionally. Add the lamb, and cook on all sides until brown. Add the remaining vegetables, then cover, and cook gently for 10 minutes. Add the sage, pour the white wine over, cover again, and cook for about 2 hours until the lamb is tender.
Lay the lamb on a heated platter, squeeze over the orange juice, and serve immediately.

Vitello al Limone
Braised Veal with Lemon

675g/1½ lb fillet of veal
seasoned flour
50g/2 oz butter
1 onion, chopped
2 carrots, chopped

1 stick of celery, chopped
a few leaves sage
300ml/½ pint Brodo di Pollo (page 30)
juice of 2 lemons

Roll the veal in the seasoned flour, then tie with string to help it keep its shape while cooking. Melt the butter in an ovenproof casserole, and brown the meat on all sides. Add the vegetables and sage, pour over the stock and half the lemon juice, then cover and cook in a moderate oven, 180°C/350°F/Gas 4, for about 2½ hours until tender. Add the remaining lemon juice about 10 minutes before the end of the cooking time.
When the meat is done, remove from the oven, carve into slices, and lay on a heated platter. Pour over the cooking juices, discarding the vegetables, and serve immediately.

Vitello al Pomodoro
Veal Cutlets in White Wine and Tomato Sauce

4 veal cutlets
seasoned flour
40g/1½ oz butter
150ml/¼ pint white wine

SAUCE
4 × 15ml spoons/4 tablespoons olive oil
1 onion, chopped
1 clove of garlic, crushed
450g/1 lb tomatoes, skinned and chopped
salt, freshly ground black pepper
6 sage leaves, finely chopped

To make the sauce, heat the oil in a pan, and gently cook the onion and garlic until soft, stirring occasionally. Add the tomatoes, seasoning and sage, and cook slowly, covered, until the sauce has thickened.

Meanwhile, flatten the cutlets with a cutlet bat or rolling-pin, then coat them in seasoned flour.

Melt the butter in a pan, and cook the cutlets briskly until browned on both sides. Pour the wine over, and cook over moderate heat until most of it has evaporated. Add the sauce, cover the pan, then cook gently for a few more minutes until the cutlets are tender.

Serve with rice, boiled potatoes or polenta (page 46).

Variation
Chicken or pork can also be cooked in this way.

Vitello al Pomodoro and *Polenta* (page 46)

Maiale al Finocchio
Pork Chops with Fennel

25g/1 oz butter
salt, freshly ground black pepper
4 pork chops
1 clove of garlic, crushed

1 × 5ml spoon/1 teaspoon fennel seeds
4 × 15ml spoons/4 tablespoons dry white
   wine

Melt the butter in a frying pan, season the chops on both sides, and fry for about 15 minutes on each side until cooked through. Transfer to a heated serving dish, and keep warm.

Add the garlic and fennel seeds to the pan, and cook until the garlic is browned, then pour the wine over. Cook quickly for 2–3 minutes until the liquid is reduced, then pour it over the chops, and serve immediately.

Costolette di Maiale al Pomodoro
Pork Chops with Tomatoes

4 × 15ml spoons/4 tablespoons olive oil
1 onion, chopped
2 cloves garlic, chopped
4 pork chops
2 × 15ml spoons/2 tablespoons white wine
   vinegar

4 × 15ml spoons/4 tablespoons dry white
   wine
350g/12 oz canned tomatoes, drained and
   sieved
1 bay leaf
salt, freshly ground black pepper
16 black olives

Heat the olive oil in a flameproof casserole large enough to hold the chops in one layer. Add the onion and garlic, and cook quickly, stirring, until they begin to brown. Add the chops, and brown on both sides. Pour over the wine vinegar and the white wine, and cook for a further 5 minutes. Add the tomatoes, bay leaf and seasoning, and turn the chops over in the sauce to coat both sides. Cover and cook over moderate heat for 30–40 minutes, adding a little water if necessary to prevent the sauce from drying out. Add the olives 10 minutes before the end of the cooking time.

Transfer the chops to a heated serving plate, spoon over the sauce and olives, and serve immediately.

Fegato di Maiale alla Fiorentina
Florentine-style Pig's Liver

2 × 15ml spoons/2 tablespoons breadcrumbs
2 cloves garlic, crushed
1 × 15ml spoon/1 tablespoon fennel seeds
450g/1 lb pig's liver, cubed
salt, freshly ground black pepper

225g/8 oz caul (see **Note**)
olive oil
lemon wedges
crostini (page 9)

Mix together the breadcrumbs, garlic and fennel seeds. Roll the liver in this mixture to coat it, then sprinkle with salt and pepper, and wrap each piece in caul. Thread the liver on to 4 skewers, and cook under a hot grill for about 8 minutes, turning occasionally and basting with olive oil. Garnish with lemon wedges and *crostini*.

Note Caul is the intestinal membrane of a lamb. It is available from specialist Italian butchers.

Zampa di Maiale alla Toscana
Tuscan-style Pig's Trotters

4 pig's trotters
salt, freshly ground black pepper
2 onions, chopped
1 stick of celery, cut into pieces
1 carrot, cut into pieces
1 bay leaf

25g/1 oz butter
1 clove of garlic, crushed
400g/14 oz canned tomatoes, drained and mashed
GARNISH
chopped parsley

Boil the trotters in a large pan of salted water with 1 onion, the celery, carrot and bay leaf for about 2 hours until tender. Remove the trotters from the pan, reserving the stock and, when they have cooled down, scrape off the meat.
Melt the butter in a flameproof casserole, and gently cook the garlic and remaining onion until soft, stirring occasionally. Add the meat, tomatoes and a little of the reserved stock. Season well, then simmer for about 10 minutes until the sauce has thickened. Sprinkle with parsley, and serve immediately accompanied by boiled or baked potatoes or polenta (page 46).

Rognone al Marsala
Kidneys in Marsala

100g/4 oz butter
450g/1 lb calf's kidneys, cut into strips
25g/1 oz flour
200ml/⅓ pint Brodo di Manzo *(page 30)*

2 × 15ml spoons/2 tablespoons Marsala
a bunch of parsley, chopped
salt, freshly ground black pepper
crostini *(page 9)*

Melt half the butter in a pan and sauté the kidneys quickly to brown them and seal in the juices. Melt the remaining butter in a flameproof casserole, stir in the flour, then gradually incorporate the stock to make a smooth sauce. Stir in the Marsala, add the kidneys, cover and cook gently for about 3 minutes until the kidneys are just cooked through. They should not be allowed to toughen. Stir in the parsley, season if necessary, and serve immediately with *crostini*.

Note If you are using kidneys of a less delicate flavour than calf's kidneys, soak them for 30 minutes–1 hour in milk before cooking and they will taste less strong.

Fegato di Vitello alla Toscana
Tuscan-style Calf's Liver

450g/1 lb calf's liver, sliced
seasoned flour
4 × 15ml spoons/4 tablespoons olive oil
a small bunch of sage leaves, chopped

GARNISH
lemon wedges

Coat the liver in the seasoned flour. Heat the oil in a frying pan, and cook the liver for about 3 minutes on each side. Add the sage leaves, and cook for a further 2 minutes each side. The liver should be still moist and pink inside, or it will be tough. Garnish with lemon wedges.

Fegato di Vitello alla Toscana and *Panzanella*
(page 84)

POULTRY & GAME

A plump tender young chicken spit-roasted with butter over a barbecue or charcoal fire is a simple favourite in Tuscany. The commonest stuffing for chicken is a knob of butter, a grinding of salt and pepper and a sprig of rosemary. Chicken is also often eaten jointed and cooked in a frying pan (*in padella*) with a selection of vegetables.

Chicken livers are always saved to be cooked separately, perhaps with scrambled eggs or in a pâté, and the other giblets, together with the head and feet, are put to good use to make stock.

Guinea-fowl is another popular farmyard bird. A relation of the pheasant, its flavour is somewhere in between that of a rabbit and a chicken.

Game of all sorts is plentiful in Tuscany, but hunters are sadly lacking in discrimination, which means that anything that flies can end up in the cooking pot.

Rabbit, pheasant and partridge can all be casseroled with wine and herbs, and black olives and sweet red peppers make a typical addition to this sort of dish.

Pollo al Marsala
Chicken with Marsala

1 chicken, jointed and cut into pieces
seasoned flour
50g/2 oz butter
2 × 15ml spoons/2 tablespoons olive oil
1 carrot, sliced
1 stick of celery, sliced
1 onion, sliced

a sprig of oregano
400g/14 oz canned tomatoes, mashed, juice
   reserved
salt, freshly ground black pepper
2 × 15ml spoons/2 tablespoons Marsala
100g/4 oz button mushrooms
100g/4 oz fresh peas

Roll the chicken pieces in seasoned flour. Heat the butter with the olive oil in a flameproof casserole, and cook the chicken until brown on all sides. Add the carrot, celery, onion, oregano and tomatoes, then season to taste, and add the Marsala. Cover and simmer gently for 45 minutes. Add the mushrooms and peas, and cook for a further 30 minutes.

Polpette di Pollo
Chicken Croquettes

The Tuscans are very good at making delicious meals from *avanzi*, leftovers. With these croquettes a little chicken goes a long way.

225g/8 oz cooked chicken, chopped
50g/2 oz prosciutto (raw Italian ham) or
   salami, chopped
1 × 15ml spoon/1 tablespoon chopped parsley
4 leaves sage, chopped

350g/12 oz stale bread, soaked and squeezed
   dry
salt, freshly ground black pepper
2–3 eggs
75–100g/3–4 oz breadcrumbs
oil for deep frying

Put the chicken, *prosciutto* and herbs in a bowl and crumble over the bread. Season well, and mix very thoroughly. Add the eggs one at a time, and mash them into the mixture to bind it together.
Divide the mixture into small lumps, and roll each one into fat sausage shapes. Roll the croquettes in breadcrumbs, then deep fry in hot oil until golden. Lift them out with a slotted spoon, drain on absorbent kitchen paper, and arrange on a heated platter. Serve immediately.

Pollo alla Cacciatora
Hunter's-style Chicken

50g/2 oz butter
2 × 15ml spoons/2 tablespoons olive oil
1 onion, chopped
1 clove of garlic, chopped
1 chicken, jointed and cut into pieces
seasoned flour

450g/1 lb tomatoes, skinned and chopped
225g/8 oz porcini (ceps), cut into pieces
1 bay leaf
salt, freshly ground black pepper
4 × 15ml spoons/4 tablespoons white wine
crostini (page 9)

Heat together the butter and oil in an ovenproof casserole, and cook the onion and garlic for a few minutes until soft, stirring occasionally.
Roll the chicken pieces in seasoned flour, then add them to the casserole, and brown on all sides. Add the tomatoes, *porcini* and bay leaf, season to taste, then pour the wine over. Cover and cook slowly over moderate heat or in a warm oven, 160°C/325°F/Gas 3, for about 1 hour.
Serve with *crostini*.

Pollo Fritto alla Toscana
Tuscan-style Fried Chicken

1 chicken, jointed
MARINADE
4 × 15ml spoons/4 tablespoons olive oil
juice of 1 lemon
salt, freshly ground black pepper

1 bunch of parsley, chopped
2 eggs, beaten
seasoned flour
oil for frying

To make the marinade, mix together the oil, lemon juice, salt, pepper and parsley.
Put the chicken pieces in a deep dish and pour the marinade over. Cover and leave for 2 hours. Remove the chicken pieces with a slotted spoon, dip them in the beaten egg, then coat in the flour.
Heat some oil in a deep frying pan, and cook the chicken over moderate heat for 30–50 minutes, according to the size of the pieces, until golden and crispy on the outside and cooked through. Remove from the pan, drain on absorbent paper, arrange on a hot platter, and serve with a green salad.

Pollo alla Cacciatora

Pollo alla Diavola
Devilled Chicken

This simple dish is best cooked over a barbecue for an outdoor meal in summer.

1 chicken
MARINADE
150ml/¼ pint olive oil

2 small hot red peppers, chopped
salt, freshly ground black pepper

Split the chicken through the breastbone, open it out, then press it flat.
To make the marinade, mix the oil and chopped peppers, and
season with salt and pepper.
Lay the chicken in a dish and pour over the marinade. Let it soak up the
flavours for about 30 minutes, then cook over a barbecue for about 30
minutes, turning until done.

Pernici Ripieni
Stuffed Partridges

2 partridges, with their livers
salt, freshly ground black pepper
4 slices pancetta (bacon), chopped
50g/2 oz prosciutto (raw Italian ham),
  chopped

100g/4 oz mushrooms, chopped
4 slices Italian bread, soaked and squeezed
  out
1 egg
50g/2 oz butter

Season the partridges inside and out with salt and pepper.
Chop the livers with half the pancetta, and put in a bowl with the prosciutto
and mushrooms. Crumble in the bread, then add the egg and seasoning,
and mix well.
Stuff the partridges with this mixture, then wrap the birds in the remaining
slices of pancetta. Put them in a roasting tin, dot with the butter, and cook in
a fairly hot oven, 200°C/400°F/Gas 6, for about 40 minutes until tender.

Quaglie al Brandy
Quail with Brandy

8 quail
salt, freshly ground black pepper
2 × 15ml spoons/2 tablespoons olive oil
8 strips fat pancetta (bacon)
1 clove of garlic, crushed

1 small onion, finely chopped
a few leaves sage
150ml/¼ pint Brodo di Pollo (page 30)
150ml/¼ pint white wine
2 × 15ml spoons/2 tablespoons brandy

Season the quail with salt and pepper. Heat the olive oil in a flameproof casserole, and quickly brown the quail on all sides. Remove from the casserole, then wrap a strip of *pancetta* round each quail. Put to one side.
Add the garlic and onion to the casserole, and cook, stirring, until brown.
Add the quail and sage, then pour the stock and wine over. Reduce the heat, cover and cook for about 20 minutes.
Pour the brandy over the quail, and ignite. When the flames have died down, arrange the quail on a heated serving plate, and spoon over the cooking juices.
Serve with rice and a green salad.

Faraona in Casseruola
Casseroled Guinea-fowl

2 small guinea-fowl
salt, freshly ground black pepper
50g/2 oz butter
1 clove of garlic, crushed
100g/4 oz pancetta (bacon), chopped

a few sage and basil leaves
a sprig of rosemary
2 × 15ml spoons/2 tablespoons Marsala
150ml/¼ pint Brodo di Pollo (page 30)

Sprinkle the guinea-fowl inside and out with salt and pepper.
Melt the butter in a flameproof casserole, and gently cook the garlic and *pancetta* for about 5 minutes, stirring occasionally. Add the herbs, put in the guinea-fowl, and cook until brown on all sides. Pour the Marsala and stock over, cover, then simmer for about 1 hour until tender.
Remove the birds from the casserole, carve them, and arrange the meat on a heated platter. Spoon over a little of the sauce, and serve the rest separately.

Note Fried polenta (page 46) makes a good accompaniment to this dish.

EGGS & CHEESE

Eggs and cheese are eaten in Tuscany at all times of the day. A new-laid egg simply fried in green olive oil and with a clove of fresh garlic can be enjoyed for breakfast with a hunk of crusty bread. Eggs can be scrambled with chicken livers, chestnuts or anchovy fillets. Beaten in batter, they can be poured over sliced vegetables and baked in the oven.

The most common cheeses in Tuscany are *pecorino*, the sheep's cheese; *ricotta*, a crumbly, creamy white cheese made from ewe's milk; and Parmesan, the very hard well-matured cheese used for grating. The generic name for Parmesan is *grana*, referring to its fine grained texture. It is not a good idea to buy it ready grated as this tends to be dusty and tasteless. A large hunk of Parmesan cheese will keep for a very long time in a cool larder or in the bottom drawer of a refrigerator.

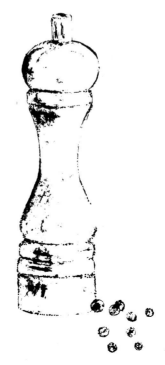

Omelette di Pasta
Pasta Omelet

Serves 1

Make this omelet using leftover cooked pasta.

75g/3 oz cooked pasta, with sauce
3 eggs
salt, freshly ground black pepper

1 × 15ml spoon/1 tablespoon finely chopped
  parsley
2 × 15ml spoons/2 tablespoons olive oil
Parmesan cheese, grated

Put the pasta and its sauce into a bowl, and chop very finely. Add the eggs, and beat well. Season with salt and pepper, then add the parsley.
Heat the olive oil in a small heavy-based pan. Pour in the egg mixture, and cook briskly until half set, moving the outside of the omelet into the middle with a wooden spoon or spatula as it cooks. Sprinkle with Parmesan cheese, then cook for a further minute. Fold the omelet in half, and slide on to a heated plate. Leave for a few seconds for the eggs to finish cooking – the omelet should still be runny inside.

Frittata alle Cipolle
Onion Omelet

40g/1½ oz butter
150g/5 oz onions, finely chopped
6 eggs
2 × 15ml spoons/2 tablespoons chopped
  parsley

salt, freshly ground black pepper
a pinch of grated nutmeg
2 × 15ml spoons/2 tablespoons olive oil

Melt the butter in a heavy-based pan, and gently cook the onion without browning until soft.
Beat the eggs lightly with the parsley, salt, pepper and nutmeg. Stir in the onion when cooked.
Add the oil to the pan and, when hot, pour in the egg mixture. Cook rapidly until golden on the outside. Remove the pan from the heat before the omelet is set, divide into 4, and serve immediately on hot plates.

Uova Strapazzate con Acciughe
Scrambled Eggs with Anchovy Fillets

50g/2 oz butter
8 eggs, beaten
4 anchovy fillets, soaked, drained and
  chopped

Cayenne pepper
crostini (page 9)

Melt the butter in a heavy-based frying pan until bubbling, then add the eggs and anchovy fillets. Cook, stirring, over moderate heat, then remove the pan from the heat before the eggs have set. Sprinkle with Cayenne pepper, and serve at once on hot plates with *crostini*.

Uova alla Fiorentina
Florentine-style Eggs

900g/2 lb spinach, washed, stalks and
  discoloured leaves discarded
25g/1 oz butter
150ml/¼ pint double cream
salt, freshly ground black pepper

4 × 15ml spoons/4 tablespoons grated
  Parmesan cheese
8 eggs
300ml/½ pint Salsa Besciamella (page 31),
  made with Parmesan cheese

Cram the spinach into a pan, cover and cook in the water clinging to the leaves for about 5 minutes, stirring occasionally. The spinach should still be bright green in colour. Press out the excess water, drain well and chop roughly.
Melt the butter in a pan, add the spinach and cream and season well. Cook gently for a couple of minutes.
Cover the bottom of a wide ovenproof dish with the spinach mixture, and sprinkle with half the Parmesan cheese. Make 8 hollows for the eggs to sit in.
Break the eggs, one by one, into a cup to check that they are fresh, then slide them into the hollows. Pour over the sauce, and sprinkle the remaining Parmesan cheese on top. Cook in a moderate oven, 180°C/350°F/Gas 4, for about 15 minutes until the eggs are just set. Serve at once.

Soufflé ai Piselli
Soufflé with Peas

Make sure your friends are sitting at the table ready to eat the soufflé immediately it is taken from the oven. If it is kept waiting, it will subside past its puffy golden best.

275g/10 oz canned marrowfat peas, drained
300ml/½ pint Salsa Besciamella *(page 31)*
50g/2 oz prosciutto (Italian raw ham), finely chopped

4 eggs, separated
butter
Parmesan cheese, grated

Mash the peas with a fork and combine well with the sauce; alternatively mix the two in a blender. Stir in the *prosciutto* and yolks.
Whisk the whites until they form soft peaks, then stir two tablespoons into the thick sauce. Lightly fold in the rest with a large metal spoon, using a figure-of-eight motion.
Tip the mixture into a buttered 20–22.5cm/8–9 inch soufflé dish sprinkled with Parmesan cheese, and bake in a fairly hot oven, 200°C/400°F/Gas 6, for about 25 minutes until well risen and golden-brown. The soufflé should not wobble as it is taken from the oven, nor should it be set rigid and dry. Serve immediately.

Uova con Fontina
Baked Eggs with Fontina Cheese

25g/1 oz butter
4 eggs
salt, freshly ground black pepper

1 large slice of prosciutto *(raw Italian ham), cut into 4*
75g/3 oz Fontina cheese, thinly sliced
4 × 15ml spoons/4 tablespoons white wine

Divide the butter between 4 ramekin dishes, and break an egg into each. Season with salt and pepper, then top each with a slice of *prosciutto* and a slice of cheese. Pour 1 × 15ml spoon/1 tablespoon white wine into each dish, and bake in a fairly hot oven, 200°C/400°F/Gas 6, for about 5 minutes until the cheese has melted and the eggs are just set. Serve immediately.

Formaggio Fritto
Cheese Fritters

400g/14 oz Fontina, Mozzarella or Gruyère
    cheese, cubed
seasoned flour

2 eggs, beaten
150g/5 oz stale white breadcrumbs (approx)
oil for deep frying

Roll the cubes of cheese first in the seasoned flour, then in the egg and finally in the breadcrumbs, coating them as evenly as possible. Deep fry in hot oil in batches in a wire basket. Remove from the oil as soon as the crumb crust is crispy and golden. Drain on absorbent paper, and keep warm until all the cubes have been fried. Serve immediately, with
Salsa di Pomodoro (page 32), if liked.

Crocchette di Mozzarella
Mozzarella Croquettes

225g/8 oz very fresh Mozzarella cheese
50g/2 oz flour
1 egg, beaten

a pinch of salt
olive oil for frying

Put the cheese in a bowl, and knead it with your hands until soft. Add about a quarter of the flour, the egg and salt, and combine well. Pull off small pieces, and shape them into fat sausage shapes. Roll the croquettes in the remaining flour, then shallow fry in hot oil until golden. Lift them out with a slotted spoon, drain on absorbent kitchen paper, and serve at once on their own or with *Salsa di Pomodoro* (page 32).

Uova con Fontina (page 75), Formaggio Fritto
and Insalata Mista (page 83)

VEGETABLES & SALADS

In Italy the vegetable course is called a *contorno*, a contour. It can be served at the side of a dish of fish or meat, or to round it off afterwards. Many of the main dishes, too, are based on vegetables – in Tuscany stuffed vegetables of all kinds are very popular.

Of most importance in preparing a vegetable dish is that it should be fresh and served in its own season so that it is as tender, young and flavoursome as possible. Certain varieties can, of course, be preserved for the winter. Beans and wild mushrooms are dried; tomatoes, essential in the kitchen all year round, are bottled or made into a sauce; artichoke hearts, olives and peppers are put under oil.

A Tuscan speciality is a salad of wild plants gathered from the fields and hedgerows. To collect these, it is important to be accompanied by a local person familiar with them. For such people, this salad is free, but in a city restaurant its novelty value makes it one of the most expensive dishes on the menu. It is not included in this book since the plants are either not available or particularly hard to find.

Spinaci in Padella
Pan-cooked Spinach

1.35kg/3 lb spinach, washed, stalks and discoloured leaves discarded
4 × 15ml spoons/4 tablespoons olive oil

2 cloves garlic, crushed
salt, freshly ground black pepper

Cram the spinach into a saucepan, cover and cook gently in only the water clinging to the leaves for about 8 minutes until it has collapsed but still retains its bright emerald green colour. Drain thoroughly, pressing out all the excess water, then chop roughly.

Heat the oil in a pan, and cook the garlic until brown. Stir in the spinach, season well, then cook for a few minutes until all the oil has been absorbed and the spinach is hot through. Serve immediately.

Crespelle alla Fiorentina
Florentine-style Pancakes

175g/6 oz plain flour
a pinch of salt
2 eggs
450ml/¾ pint milk
1 × 15ml spoon/1 tablespoon olive oil
300ml/½ pint Salsa Besciamella (page 31),
   flavoured with nutmeg

FILLING
900g/2 lb spinach, washed, stalks and
   discoloured leaves discarded
225g/8 oz Ricotta cheese
salt, freshly ground black pepper

Sift the flour into a large bowl with the salt. Make a well in the centre and add the eggs. Add half the milk very gradually, beating the liquid with a fork so that the flour slowly gets incorporated. Spoon in the oil, then continue until all the milk has been used up and the batter is thin and smooth. Leave to stand for 1 hour.

Meanwhile, prepare the filling. Cook the spinach gently in the water clinging to the leaves for about 5 minutes until it has collapsed but still retains its bright emerald green colour. It should not be allowed to go black and sludgy. Press out all the water, drain well and chop. Mix together with the Ricotta cheese and seasoning.

Heat a small heavy-based pan, pour in a very little oil and swirl it round. When the oil is hot, spoon in enough batter to coat thinly the base of the pan. Cook for about 1 minute on each side until the pancake is just beginning to turn golden. Keep each pancake warm until all the batter has been used up.

Divide the spinach mixture between the pancakes, roll up and fit into an oblong ovenproof dish. Pour over the *Salsa Besciamella*, and heat through in a moderate oven, 180°C/350°F/Gas 4, for 20 minutes. Serve immediately.

Zucchini Ripieni
Stuffed Courgettes

4 medium courgettes
2 × 15ml spoons/2 tablespoons olive oil
1 small onion, finely chopped
1 clove of garlic, crushed
2 × 15ml spoons/2 tablespoons chopped
 parsley

2 × 15ml spoons/2 tablespoons grated
 Parmesan cheese
2 slices Italian bread, soaked and squeezed
 out
salt, freshly ground black pepper
200ml/⅓ pint Salsa di Pomodoro (page 32)

Cut both ends off the courgettes, and hollow out with an apple corer. Chop
and reserve the pulp.
Heat the oil in a pan, and gently cook the onion and garlic until soft, stirring
occasionally. Transfer to a bowl with the courgette pulp, parsley and
Parmesan cheese. Crumble in the bread, season to taste, and mix well. Use to
stuff the courgettes.
Cover the bottom of a shallow casserole with the *Salsa di Pomodoro*, and
arrange the courgettes on top. Cover and cook in a fairly hot oven, 190°C/
375°F/Gas 5, for 40 minutes until all the courgettes are
tender. Serve immediately.

Finocchi Gratinati
Fennel in Cheese Sauce

2 bulbs fennel, sliced
salt
300ml/½ pint Salsa Besciamella (page 31),
 flavoured with nutmeg

2 × 15ml spoons/2 tablespoons grated
 Parmesan cheese
2 × 15ml spoons/2 tablespoons dried
 breadcrumbs

Cook the fennel in boiling salted water until tender, then drain well. Arrange
in an ovenproof serving dish, and pour over the *Salsa Besciamella*. Sprinkle
with the Parmesan cheese and breadcrumbs, and brown quickly under a hot
grill. Serve at once.

Fiori di Zucchini Ripieni
Stuffed Courgette Flowers

Serve these as an appetizer or a vegetable. Combined with other stuffed vegetables, such as courgettes, tomatoes and peppers, they make a meal in themselves.

8 courgette flowers (see **Note***)*
1 egg, beaten
seasoned flour
oil for deep frying
STUFFING
4 slices Italian bread (approx), soaked, squeezed out and crumbled

a pinch of dried oregano
1 egg yolk
2 × 15ml spoons/2 tablespoons grated Parmesan cheese
1–2 slices prosciutto (raw Italian ham), finely diced
salt, freshly ground black pepper

Prepare the stuffing first. Combine the ingredients for the stuffing, then spoon the mixture into the courgette flowers. Dip first in the beaten egg, then in the seasoned flour, and deep fry in hot oil until golden. Drain on absorbent paper, and serve at once.

Note The flower of the courgette plant precedes the appearance of the courgette vegetable.

Tortino di Carciofi alla Toscana
Tuscan-style Artichoke Bake

6 young artichokes, soaked for 1 hour in acidulated water
150ml/¼ pint olive oil (approx)
seasoned flour
8 eggs
2 × 15ml spoons/2 tablespoons milk

2 × 15ml spoons/ 2 tablespoons grated Pecorino cheese
2 × 15ml spoons/2 tablespoons grated Parmesan cheese
salt, freshly ground black pepper

Trim away the tough outer leaves and the stalks of the artichokes, then cut them vertically into slices.
Heat the olive oil in a pan, dip the artichoke slices in the seasoned flour, and fry on both sides until golden. Drain on absorbent paper, then lay in the base of a wide ovenproof dish.
Beat the eggs with the milk, Pecorino and Parmesan cheeses, and season well. Pour the batter over the artichokes, and bake in a warm oven, 160°C/325°F/ Gas 3, for about 15 minutes or until just set but not hard. Serve at once.

Fondi di Carciofi alla Fiorentina
Florentine-style Artichoke Hearts

8 artichokes (see **Note**)
lemon juice or white wine vinegar
900g/2 lb spinach, washed, stalks and
   discoloured leaves discarded
40g/1½ oz butter
1 onion, finely chopped
75g/3 oz prosciutto (raw Italian ham), diced

salt, freshly ground black pepper
300ml/½ pint Salsa Besciamella (page 31)
   using 1 egg yolk and nutmeg
4 × 15ml spoons/4 tablespoons breadcrumbs
4 × 15ml spoons/4 tablespoons grated
   Parmesan cheese

To prepare the artichoke hearts, simply dismantle the artichokes with a very sharp knife. Cut off the leaves and the stalk, and scrape away the choke. Put the artichoke hearts in acidulated water until you are ready to use them. Cook for about 5 minutes in boiling acidulated water until tender, then drain and put to one side.

Meanwhile, cram the spinach in a saucepan, cover and cook gently for about 8 minutes in only the water clinging to the leaves. Drain well and chop roughly.

Melt the butter in a pan, and cook the onion until brown, stirring occasionally. Stir in the *prosciutto* and spinach, season well, and cook, stirring, for a couple of minutes until all the butter has been absorbed.

Put the spinach in a layer in the base of a wide ovenproof dish. Arrange the artichoke hearts on top, and cover with the *Salsa Besciamella*. Sprinkle with the breadcrumbs and Parmesan cheese, and bake in a fairly hot oven, 190°C/375°F/Gas 5, for about 20 minutes until golden-brown and crisp on top. Serve at once.

Note If fresh artichokes are not available, use canned artichoke hearts.

Carciofi Farciti
Stuffed Artichokes

4 artichokes, soaked for 1 hour in acidulated
 water
lemon juice
salt, freshly ground black pepper
100g/4 oz Ricotta cheese
2 × 15ml spoons/2 tablespoons grated
 Parmesan cheese

50g/2 oz prosciutto (raw Italian ham), diced
2 × 15ml spoons/2 tablespoons pine nut
 kernels
2 × 15ml spoons/2 tablespoons breadcrumbs
2 × 15ml spoons/2 tablespoons chopped
 parsley

Trim away the tough outer leaves of the artichokes, and cut the stalk off
neatly so that the artichoke stands up on its base. Slice across the top of the
artichoke, ready to form a cup. Rub the cut edges in lemon juice to stop them
going brown. Boil the artichokes in salted acidulated water for about 30
minutes. To test if they are ready, tug at one of the outer leaves. If it will
come away easily, the artichokes are cooked. Drain them
upside-down, and leave to cool.
Pull out the centre leaves of the artichokes, and scrape
away the choke with a teaspoon.
Mix together the remaining ingredients and season well. Use to stuff the
artichokes, and serve at once.

Insalata Mista
Mixed Salad

The simplest way to dress a fresh salad is with salt, pepper and good olive oil. There
is no need to sour the flavour by adding vinegar.

2 heads radicchio
1 yellow pepper, de-seeded and cut into strips
50g/2 oz French beans, cooked and cut into
 manageable lengths

2 large Mediterranean tomatoes, sliced
salt, freshly ground black pepper
1–2 × 15ml spoons/1–2 tablespoons olive oil

Separate the radicchio into leaves, then dry in a lettuce spinner. Alternatively,
wrap the leaves in a tea-towel and swing it round your head until all the
excess moisture has been removed.
Mix together the radicchio, pepper, beans and tomatoes in a large bowl,
sprinkle with the salt and pepper, and dribble on olive oil to taste. Toss well,
then serve.

Insalata di Finocchi e Ricotta
Fennel and Ricotta Salad

A refreshing salad that goes well with simply cooked white fish.

2 bulbs fennel, thinly sliced
225g/8 oz Ricotta cheese, crumbled
a handful of parsley, chopped

2 × 15ml spoons/ 2 tablespoons olive oil
a squeeze of lemon juice
salt, freshly ground black pepper

Mix together the fennel, Ricotta cheese and parsley in a bowl. Pour over the oil, then squeeze on the lemon juice, and season with salt and pepper. Toss well and leave to stand for about 30 minutes so that the flavours can blend.

Panzanella
Soaked Bread Salad

A tasty way of using up stale slices of coarse white Italian bread.

1 clove of garlic, halved
4 slices stale Italian bread
a handful of chopped basil and parsley, mixed
2 small pink and white onions, sliced
450g/1 lb ripe tomatoes, sliced

1 cucumber, sliced (leave the peel on)
4 × 15ml spoons/4 tablespoons olive oil
2 × 15ml spoons/2 tablespoons white wine vinegar
salt, freshly ground black pepper

Rub a salad bowl with the cut edges of the garlic.
Soak the bread briefly in water, then crumble it roughly into the bowl. Add the herbs, onions, tomatoes and cucumber.
Mix the olive oil with the vinegar, and season well. Pour this over the salad, toss well, and serve.

Insalata di Finocchi e Ricotta

DESSERTS & CAKES

Except on special occasions, a dessert in a Tuscan household will inevitably be fresh fruit and cheese. A ripe pear and a slice of *pecorino* is a simple and very satisfying way of rounding off a meal.

Feast days, and particularly religious festivals, are, however, commemorated by the baking of special cakes and pastries to be eaten at any time of the day.

The desserts in this chapter are typical of those that would be prepared in Tuscany for a celebration. Otherwise it is quite common to buy a more elaborate, very sweet and fancy-looking concoction from the *pasticceria* or to serve sweet biscuits or macaroons with strong black coffee.

Torta di Albicocche
Apricot Tart

175g/6 oz plain flour
a pinch of salt
75g/3 oz butter
1 egg yolk
2 × 15ml spoons/2 tablespoons iced water
  (approx)
450g/1 lb large ripe apricots, halved and
  stoned

1–2 × 15ml spoons/1–2 tablespoons Marsala
FILLING
300ml/½ pint double cream
2 eggs
caster sugar

Make the pastry first. Sift the flour into a bowl with the salt. Cream the butter, then add to the bowl with the egg yolk. Cut the mixture repeatedly with a knife until it forms large crumbs. Pour on the water, and mix with a knife until it begins to hold together. You may need a little more water. Form into a ball with your hands, wrap in clingfilm, and chill for 30 minutes.

Roll out the pastry on a floured surface. Fold it into four, then roll it out again. Fold it back up, form it into a ball, wrap in clingfilm, and chill for a further 30 minutes.

Roll the pastry out to 2.5–5mm/⅛–¼ inch thickness, and use to line a 20cm/8 inch greased and floured pie dish. Prick the base with a fork, and chill for a further 30 minutes.

Meanwhile, prepare the filling. Beat or whisk the cream with the eggs and sugar to taste.

Arrange the apricots in the chilled pastry case, cut side down. Sprinkle with the Marsala, then bake in a fairly hot oven, 200°C/400°F/Gas 6, for 10 minutes to firm up. Pour over the cream mixture, return to the oven, and cook for about 30 minutes until set and golden on top. Leave to cool, then serve warm or cold.

Zucotto
Florentine Dessert Cake

The name of this dessert means 'little pumpkin'. It is made in a rounded mould and
decorated like a golf umbrella with alternate segments of cocoa powder
and icing sugar.

50g/2 oz shelled hazelnuts
50g/2 oz almonds, chopped
450g/1 lb sponge or Madeira cake
4 × 15ml spoons/4 tablespoons brandy
4 × 15ml spoons/4 tablespoons sweet liqueur
600ml/1 pint whipping cream

100g/4 oz icing sugar, sifted
100g/4 oz bitter chocolate, grated
DECORATION
cocoa powder, sifted
icing sugar

Put the hazelnuts on a baking sheet, and toast in a hot oven, 220°C/425°F/Gas
7, for 5 minutes. Leave to cool slightly, then rub off the skins and chop
coarsely. Mix with the almonds.

Cut the cake into slices or fingers, and soak in the brandy and liqueur. Use
about half to line a 1.8 litre/3 pint flattish pudding basin.

Whip the cream with the icing sugar until stiff, then fold in the chopped nuts
and the chocolate.

Fill the basin with the cream mixture, and cover with the remaining cake.
Cover the basin with clingfilm, then chill for several hours.

Remove the clingfilm and invert a flat-bottomed plate over the mould. Turn
out, and decorate the top with cocoa powder and icing sugar in alternate
segments. Serve immediately.

Zucotto

Crostata di Ricotta
Ricotta Cheesecake

175g/6 oz plain flour
a pinch of salt
75g/3 oz butter
1 egg yolk
2 × 15ml spoons/2 tablespoons iced water
   (approx)

FILLING
450g/1 lb Ricotta cheese
100g/4 oz caster sugar
25g/1 oz raisins
25g/1 oz sultanas
grated rind of 1 lemon
2 × 15ml spoons/2 tablespoons Marsala

To make the pastry, sift the flour into a bowl with the salt. Cream the butter, then add to the bowl with the egg yolk. Cut the mixture repeatedly with a knife until it forms large crumbs. Pour on the water, and mix with a knife until it begins to hold together. Form into a ball with your hands, wrap in clingfilm, and chill for 30 minutes.

Roll out the pastry on a floured surface, fold it into four, then roll it out again. Fold it back up, form it into a ball, wrap in clingfilm, and chill for a further 30 minutes.

Roll the pastry out to 2.5–5mm/⅛–¼ inch thickness, and use to line a greased and floured 20cm/8 inch loose-bottomed flan tin. Bake blind in a moderate oven, 180°C/350°F/Gas 4, for 15 minutes.

Meanwhile, mix together the ingredients for the filling.

Remove the base from the oven, and spread the filling into it evenly. Return to the oven for 30–40 minutes until the filling is set and a cocktail stick inserted in the centre comes out dry. Leave to cool, then remove the sides of the tin. Serve cold.

Ricotta al Caffè
Ricotta with Coffee

The Ricotta should be very fresh. Have a bowl of fruit on the table to complement the creaminess of this rich but simple dessert.

225g/8 oz Ricotta cheese
2 × 15ml spoons/2 tablespoons ground coffee

2 × 15ml spoons/2 tablespoons caster sugar

Cream the Ricotta with the coffee, and form into four small mounds. Set each one on a small plate. Sprinkle with the sugar, and serve.

Cenci alla Fiorentina
Deep-fried Sweet Pastry

Cenci – the name means 'tatters' – are a speciality of Lucca and a particular favourite with children. They are strips of sweet pastry, tied in knots or bows and deep-fried until they puff up.

225g/8 oz flour
2 eggs plus 2 egg yolks
2 × 15ml spoons/2 tablespoons rum

25g/1 oz caster sugar plus *extra for dredging*
a pinch of salt
oil for deep frying

Sift 175g/6 oz flour into a bowl, make a well in the centre, then add the eggs, yolks, rum, sugar and salt. Mix with a fork until all the flour has been incorporated. Form the mixture into a soft dough with your hands.
Sift the remaining flour on to a pastry board, and knead the dough for about 5 minutes until all the flour has been incorporated and the dough is smooth.
Leave to rest for 30 minutes, covered with a damp tea-towel.
Cut off one-quarter of the dough at a time, and roll it out thinly on a floured surface. Cut into strips about 1.25cm/¼ inch wide and 15cm/6 inches long, then tie a loose knot in each strip, and deep fry in hot oil, a few at a time, until golden-brown and puffy. Remove the *cenci* with a slotted spoon, and drain on absorbent paper. Continue until all the dough has been used up. Dredge with caster sugar, and serve immediately.

Granita di Fragole
Strawberry Water Ice

Ices have been popular in Italy since Roman times, when snow was brought down from the mountains and flavoured with crushed fruit and honey.

450g/1 lb strawberries, hulled
100g/4 oz caster sugar

150ml/¼ pint water
juice of 1 orange

Press the strawberries through a sieve or purée them in a blender.
Put the sugar and water into a small heavy-based pan, and stir over low heat until syrupy. Mix with the strawberry purée and orange juice, then pour into a shallow freezer tray, and freeze for about 3 hours until set.
Spoon the *granita* into sorbet glasses, and chill until required.

Prugne alla Grappa
Prunes in Grappa

A delicious Christmas treat.

prunes, washed and dried   *Grappa*
a vanilla pod

Pack the prunes tightly in a screw-topped jar, and pack the vanilla pod in amongst them. Cover with the Grappa, screw the lid on tightly, and store in a cool, dark, dry place for at least 2 months.

Panforte di Siena
Siennese Spice Cake

100g/4 oz slivered almonds   *275g/10 oz candied peel*
100g/4 oz hazelnuts, chopped   *3 × 15ml spoons/3 tablespoons honey*
1 × 5ml spoon/1 teaspoon ground cinnamon   *50g/2 oz caster sugar*
1 × 5ml spoon/1 teaspoon grated nutmeg   *DECORATION*
50g/2 oz self-raising flour   *icing sugar*

Mix together thoroughly the nuts, spices, flour and candied peel.
Put the honey and sugar in a large heavy-based pan, and cook gently, stirring, until a little of the mixture dropped into a glass of cold water forms a ball.
Add the cake mixture to the pan, and stir well.
Transfer the mixture to a greased and floured 20cm/ 8 inch loose-bottomed flan tin, and cook in a cool oven, 150°C/300°F/Gas 2, for 30 minutes until a skewer inserted in the centre comes out clean. Leave to cool slightly, then remove the sides of the tin, and dredge the top with icing sugar. Leave to cool completely, then cut into slices. Serve with coffee.

Pane Toscano
Tuscan Bread

25g/1 oz fresh yeast or 1 × 15ml spoon/
1 tablespoon dried yeast
300ml/½ pint warm water (approx)
450g/1 lb strong white flour

1 × 15ml spoon/1 tablespoon olive oil plus
a little to paint the top of the loaf
a sprinkling of rosemary needles (optional)

Blend the fresh yeast into enough warm water to cover, or reconstitute the dried yeast as directed on the packet. Leave in a warm place until the yeast is really frothy – this may take about 15 minutes.

Sift the flour into a large bowl and mix in the oil. Add the yeast liquid and enough of the remaining warm water to make a soft and pliable dough.

Turn on to a floured surface, and knead for about 10 minutes until smooth, elastic and no longer sticky. (If you are using a dough hook on a mixer, 1–2 minutes will suffice.) Place the dough in a large lightly oiled polythene bag, and leave in a warm place until it has risen so far that it will rise no more. Leave it overnight if convenient.

Slap back the dough to knock out the air, and form into a flattened round or oval shape on an oiled baking sheet. Brush the top with olive oil, and sprinkle with rosemary needles, if liked. Cover with a sheet of oiled polythene and leave in a warm place for about 1 hour or until it will rise no more.

Bake in a very hot oven, 230°C/450°F/Gas 8, for 10 minutes, then reduce the heat to fairly hot, 190°C/375°F/Gas 5, and bake for a further 20 minutes until the loaf is crisp on the outside and sounds hollow when tapped on the bottom. Return it to the oven if necessary for a few more minutes. Cool on a wire rack.

MENUS

Lunch is the main meal of the day – a family affair. It begins with or is centred round a bowl of pasta, a thick soup or a risotto. This substantial first course can be followed by simply grilled or roast meat or fish, flavoured with olive oil, herbs, and sometimes garlic, to be rounded off with fresh fruit and cheese.

On a Sunday or other feast day, the meal might start with antipasti, then a pasta dish, followed by a meat, poultry or fish dish, and ending with a dessert such as a fruit tart and a heavy spicy cake. Such a meal might well be rounded off with home-produced *vin santo*, a sweet strong wine kept for special occasions.

Lunch Menu

Minestra di Pasta e Fagioli (page 21)

•

Pollo Fritto alla Toscana (page 68)

•

Insalata di Finocchi e Ricotta (page 84)

•

Fresh Fruit and Cheese

Celebration Menu

Funghi Ripieni (page 15)

•

Tagliatelle Paglia e Fieno (page 35)

•

Agnello al Vino Bianco (page 59)

•

Spinaci in Padella (page 78)

•

Torta di Albicocche (page 87)

Sunday Menu

Polenta Teneri alla Livornese (page 47)

•

Triglie al Prosciutto (page 52)

•

Ricotta al Caffè (page 90)

INDEX